# The
# HEIRLOOM
# HOUSE

## HOW EBAY AND I
## DECORATED AND FURNISHED
## MY NANTUCKET HOME

### SHERRY LEFEVRE

Skyhorse Publishing

Skyhorse Publishing books may be purchased in bulk at special discounts for sales promotion, corporate gifts, fund-raising, or educational purposes. Special editions can also be created to specifications. For details, contact the Special Sales Department, Skyhorse Publishing, 307 West 36th Street, 11th Floor, New York, NY 10018 or info@skyhorsepublishing.com

Skyhorse® and Skyhorse Publishing® are registered trademarks of Skyhorse Publishing, Inc.®, a Delaware corporation.

Visit our website at www.skyhorsepublishing.com.

10 9 8 7 6 5 4 3 2 1

Library of Congress Cataloging-in-Publication Data is available on file.

Cover design by Erin Seaward-Hiatt

Cover photo provided by Sherry Lefevre

Interior design and illustrations by Ryan Penn

Print ISBN: 978-1-63450-233-7

Ebook ISBN: 978-1-5107-0077-2

Printed in China

*To my parents*
*Lil and Tom Lefevre*
*who, along with everything else,*
*gave me Nantucket*

Thank you to the Nantucket Historic Association and to Laurie Robertson for contributing on-site photographs.

Special thanks to Linda George for her true partnership in bringing this book to light: promoting, proofing, and lovingly prodding me along. Best Friends Forever.

# TABLE OF CONTENTS

*Introduction*

I always longed to inherit an old wind-battered, wonky-floored summer house, but I didn't. I dreamed of being shepherded into an attic one Sunday afternoon by a spotted, aging aunt, breathless and palsied but eager to reveal the hidden treasures of a checkered past that would soon become my inheritance: snuff boxes, tea caddies, needlepoint samplers, folksy whirligigs, and miniature portraits (on ivory) of rakish great uncles. But I had no aunts, no attics,

A nineteenth-century cottage.

and no one in my family happened to own anything but a 1960s Rancher.

I grew up in Philadelphia's blue-blood suburbs—the Main Line—where my classmates had grandmothers with cabins in the Adirondacks and the Great Lakes, or oceanfront properties in Northeast Harbor and Prouts Neck, Maine. The calendar read 1963, but my prep school classmates still called boots Wellingtons, raincoats Macintoshes, and record players Victrolas because their summer houses contained

Sherry Lefevre

these things. Being newcomers from Florida, my family called things what sales people in department stores called them. And they bought whatever version of raincoat was the least expensive (not durable) because in their hometown, St. Petersburg, Florida, people simply died; they didn't live on forever in their heirlooms.

So it's highly likely that I developed my coveting impulses from being a child on the margin of inclusion, a child always two or three name brands removed from her peers. Psychologists encourage this kind of self-awareness, and I'm happy to oblige, but this book is a testimonial to my own personal credo—which is that you should never take the fun out of being dys*func*tional.

That being the case, I spent my early twenties cluttering my apartments with bits of broken blue-and-white china, threw an old quilt over the seat cushions on my standard-issue, Haitian-cotton sofa, and watched from the sidelines as retail home furnishings caught up with me.

The Archangel of my kindred spirits was Ralph Lauren, of course. When, in 1982, he unveiled his first line of blue-blood home furnishings, leather suitcases and trunks full of camp blankets and herringbone riding jackets, it began to seem possible that anyone could be to-the-manor-born. Moreover, you could pick your bloodline, by region even. Freed from the shackles of a legitimate heritage, you could inherit, by credit card, a hunting lodge in Southwest Utah, complete with Aztec Indian style blankets and deerskin jackets or a shingled house on the coast of Maine complete with walking sticks and needlepoint pillows. But it took a lot of new money to buy the old moneyed look. Which, well, once again I didn't have.

And then, in 2003, I discovered eBay.

eBay was the stairway to the attic of my dreams. eBay made inheritance possible through adoption—of other people's unwanted inheritance.

Given the yin and yang of the world, why was I surprised to find how many people want to unburden themselves of their great aunt's clutter? My fantasy of a room filled with odd mint tins, Victorian needle cases, perfume bottles, family tintypes, scratchy homespun and civil war journals is, it turns out, someone else's nightmare.

Indeed, on reflection, I realized I had a friend for whom Biedermeier furniture is yet another cross she has to bear for being married to a man who inherited it from German grandparents. While I found happy kinship with a family that crated up and shipped out grandfather's ivory inlaid secretary before hitting the ground running from Nazi persecution.

The first thing I ever bought on eBay was, however, not a family heirloom. It was a stuffed gorilla that rocked from side to side, played bongo drums, and sang "I don't wanna work, I just wanna bang on the drums all day." My son had been given this slice of heaven for his birthday and I observed the shy envy of his cousin, his smile always a little too taut, as he pressed its "on" switch over and over again. I wanted to buy him one for Christmas. But I couldn't find it anywhere. "Did you try eBay?" someone from the twenty-first century suggested. So I opened the site and typed in "gorilla bongo drums sings" and *poof,* there he was. For $5 plus shipping. It was like Disney magic. Bibbedy boppedy boo, and my little nephew's dream came true.

And then I asked myself the inevitable, fateful eBay Pandora's box of a question: could my own little materialistic dreams come true as well? So I typed in "rubber cigar with blowout worm" and *poof*; then I typed in "vintage pinecone elf with lantern" and *poof*; then I typed in "vintage Rushton Zippy monkey" and *poof*.

Initially, the fact that I was no longer eleven didn't occur to me. Thinking of my nephew, I was in a rush to fulfill all the painfully pent-up longings of my disadvantaged (because denied something) childhood. Two Christmases in a row I had asked for Zippy the rubber-faced chimpanzee doll. The cool cigar with blow-out worm had broken within minutes of its life with me. These wounds must have been throbbing just below the surface of my fortitude because at the mere hint of a salve, they had come

screaming through my synapses, channeling down into my racing fingertips.

Moreover, the purveyors of this eBay magic knew precisely what they were doing because there, in front of me, under a gelatinous smiling Zip, complete with overalls and beanie, were these words:

"I've been listing my entire lifetime Zippy monkey collection, wanting to make sure they all go to the right people . . . people who had one as a child, who lost him and want him back, or people who were never lucky enough to have one."

Through the magic of eBay, you could resurrect your childhood, and make it right; you could improve, repair, replace whatever chink there had been in your armor of "things I need in order to feel loved."

Fortunately I had children, albeit fully grown, inside whose birthday and Christmas and Easter and Valentine "wishes" I could smuggle what had clearly been the contraband of my childhood. And fortunately my children are both obviously better sports than I was about getting things they don't want, because, as my daughter pointed out with irritating sobriety, who could want stuffed animals called Steiff that you can't hug because they're hard and they prickle? It was an inexplicably long time before I shifted my coveting obsessions away from the 1950s and 1960s of my childhood and in the direction of a past I had never owned—the impulse, in other words, that paved the way to this book.

It started because I needed to create a guest room in my house, from scratch. Heaven be praised, there was not a stick of furniture in the space. I had never had the luxury of a room fully dedicated to welcoming outsiders. Liberated from the requirements of permanent residency, it was the perfect stage for a set redolent with connotation.

For some, wanting to make a guest room feel warm and welcoming means lace frills and scents. I've always been suspicious of scents.

I was more drawn to the great escape notion of a guest room. Maybe it's my own  run-away instinct, but I assume guests are, first and foremost, happy to escape from wherever they have come. If I could have put together a large enough tent with canteens swinging from support rods, I might have . . . or the interior of an Orient Express train car . . . or an AM/PM gas station store complete with glass-doored refrigerators . . . Instead, I created a one-room lakeside cabin in center city Philadelphia. You are supposed to imagine yourself in a very bad picture above the bed.

When I was twelve, a classmate of mine had invited me to the Ausable Club in the Adirondacks for a "play week." It was my first encounter with twig furniture and leather stitched lampshades and walls made of chocolate-colored tree trunks layered with vanilla frosting. Later in life, when Robert Redford came out with his Sundance catalogue, I scoffed at his hammered metal moose hooks. Really.

I used "antique Adirondack" as a search term on eBay. I purchased everything in the room (except the bed) on eBay. All of these nostalgic impulse purchases were good practice. They prepared me for my eBay marathon—the recovery of the greatest loss of my childhood. She was simple and sturdy, like Citizen Kane's Rosebud, companionable, like Zip the Chimp  . . .  only unfortunately much bigger.

Because she was a house.

1

*Rosemary*

From 1963 to 1966 my parents managed to push open the gate to the world of Philadelphia's **gentry**, though only temporarily. They rented a vacation house called Rosemary, in the little village of 'Sconset on Nantucket Island. That was several decades before the "uber wealthy" would mistake the foggy, windy, briar patch of an island for

The Heirloom House

the French Riviera. The ferry workers still spat chewing tobacco on the hood of your car as they directed it over the narrow ramp onto the *Nobska* (a real steamship) or the *Uncatena* (a real stinkpot). The Old Mill still had a miller and the Sankety Lighthouse still had Coast Guard lighthouse keepers.

For an eleven-year-old on a bike the island's vistas, its high bluffs, its rolling moors, its grey, shingled houses with widow's walks, confirmed my sense that fiction was more relevant than daily life. Everything around me was the setting for my summer reading list: Thomas Hardy, the Bronte sisters, Stevenson, Melville, Scott (the canon for prep schools having not yet moved beyond the nineteenth century). I had never been to a place where history was so easily imagined, and so I spent my summers happily imagining it, in a blissful solitude afforded by a sky blue Schwinn.

My two older brothers had crossed the great divide by the time we vacationed in Nantucket. They were teenagers, dating and drinking, preferring peer posses at more popular beaches to our family beach outings. We met up for meals where their frustration with everything familial expressed itself in verbal abuse, which in 1964 meant melodramatic mimicry of everything I said. We had nothing in common.

**Except, it turns out, our love for Rosemary.**

Rosemary was an early nineteenth-century white clapboard house to which a turret had been added in the late Victorian era. She sat on the Main Street of 'Sconset village, back from the road, on a lot large enough to accommodate a "secret garden" surrounded by a twenty-foot-high privet hedge whose entry arch was so overgrown it took us several weeks to discover it. Her interior was of a piece.

There was a long parlor on one side of the entry hall, with a huge horsehair sofa (a Sheraton) upholstered in deep rose-colored velvet. Next to it was a mahogany game table, which held a lamp with a frosted hurricane shade surrounded by large dangling crystals (probably American Brilliant). On the other side of the entry hall was a Damask-wallpapered study. Its pedestal desk (with olive-green tooled leather inset) offered a view of Main Street. The other three walls were lined in bookcases, each with glass doors and key locks. Every book I had ever been assigned was on those shelves or in the bookcases on the upstairs landing, or on shelves in the back "sewing" room.

Behind the study was a bedroom—my parents'—inconsequential in my memory except that it led to a back stair, a steep dark one that deposited you in an upstairs bedroom. Why? An insane wife, hidden away, her meals smuggled up the back stair? A crippled daughter (polio) who wanted the upper bedroom because of the view into the secret garden, where perhaps . . . someday . . . a suitor . . .

The kitchen and back utility room were ramshackle places that cantilevered off the back of the house with marked nonchalance, especially in view of what shrines to marble and granite our kitchens have become. Thin, flowered curtains, not doors, hid the pipes under the sink and the brooms and dustpan in the closet. Dishes, cups, pots, pans—all were stacked on open shelves and the counter-top next to the sink was wood, creviced and stained by years of watery use, like limestone rock in a canyon. The laundry equipment in the utility room included a washboard and a clothes wringer, vice clamped to a huge porcelain basin.

On the second floor, my own room was under eaves in the roof, which made the flowered wallpaper drape down over my bed like a tent. It had twin iron beds, painted white, with modest finials and a sweet interior arch. Wood floors, painted a light blue, had pale blue-and-white rag rugs that skittered like an early form of roller blade. The bedspreads were white as well, with blue and pink cotton chenille "popcorn" patterns. There was a tall, dark chest of drawers centered between the beds and the room's two windows. On that chest were things I'd never seen before—a china perfume tray for bobby pins and hair ribbons and presumably perfume bottles. A monogrammed dresser set complete with button hook and a large silver handled mirror that allowed me to see the back of my head for the first time in my entire life.

### A collar box!!!!!

By today's standards there was nothing really summery about Rosemary. Her Oriental rugs and velvet upholstery took no account of sandy feet and bathing suits. Her dark hues made no attempt to reflect light and create airiness. But in her essential other-worldliness, Rosemary was the perfect summer retreat. We were 390 miles and 150 years away from home. We were in a house where more than a century of living had left its marks, its hiding places, its scraps of play (marbles, drawings) . . . enough evidence to urge our imaginations on. Accompanied by a mise-en-scène of tempest-like storms, pitch dark, edge-of-the world skies, moor-roaming ghost-like

The Heirloom House

fog, our imaginations vacationed in lands of pirates, shipwrecks, and sea monsters—as far away from long-division and Latin case endings as we could be.

Rosemary wasn't unique in its anachronistic furnishings. Most of the island's summer home furnishings would rate the reject line at Antiques Roadshow—old but not pedigreed. In 'Sconset there were probably enough Blue Willow or Indian Tree plates to make a set, but not in any one house. Oriental rugs lacked pile and Hobnail bedspreads lacked Hobnails. Putting aside the fact that you could certainly find complete sets of Canton Rose Medallion in Newport-style houses, the consistency of the worn and mis-matched style, from the Adirondacks to Northeast Harbor to the Great Lakes to the Cape and Islands suggests that it is one of those cultural phenomena that is ideology disguised as pragmatism.

Couldn't beach house owners afford complete sets of china before the 1970s? Well, yes. But in terms of what many people budgeted as appropriate for summerhouse expenditures the answer was no. As a line item, it fell far below the year-round residence, the boarding school and college tuitions and the trust contributions.

In other words, couldn't afford was really shouldn't afford.

Thus it became a point of pride to flaunt the devaluation of summer home maintenance. During our first summer on the island in the 1960s, a club we belonged to put on a musical revue in which pretty much everyone let loose their Broadway fantasies. Included in these ranks were two of the grander "dames" of the village. They were homeowners, not renters like us, and they had the "never-mind" approach to rehearsals to prove it. But their aged, warbling voices so perfectly complemented their bird-like appearance that their duet "My House is Older Than Your House" became one of those theatrical moments when eternal truth and human history seem to elide as in an eclipse. "The house," whose wood floors and post-and-beam structure served the purpose well, thundered when they curtsied.

"My House is Older Than Your House" was a pastoral, of sorts. It was a singing contest in which the two women tried to best each other in proclaiming the virtues of their Nantucket houses. Only the brags were the opposite of what you expected.

Because consummate decrepitude was the apogee of perfection and holes in the roof, nesting bats, warped floors, leaky plumbing, were all scoring points. Here's how it went:

*Refrain: My house is older than yours,*
*my house is older than yours is.*

*My house has been through the wars*
*—has yours? Has yours? Has yours?*
*My house has beams that are old*
*—And when it rains, it's so cold here.*
*Do you have walls old with mold?*
*Behold Behold Behold*
*—My house has roses that reach to the sky*
*Windows too small to see through.*

*Refrain: My house is older than yours,*
*my house is older than yours is.*

*It's just like living outdoors*
*—Is yours? Is yours? Is yours?*

*My house has shingles galore*
*—But the shingles don't mingle together*
*Termites have eaten the door.*
*And are you keeping score?*
*My house was painted the day it was built*
*And could you ever dispute?*

*Refrain: My house is older than yours,*
*My house is older than yours is.*

The song's composers, Herb Sweet and Jack Gowen, were Broadway professionals brought in for the summer. I had visited New York for a day on my eighth birthday and had seen enough to know that their island bore little resemblance to ours. I liked to imagine what shocking encounters in Nantucket houses engendered the song's insights:

*"Did you know that one of your 'ocean views'*
*is under the sink in the bathroom?"*

*"Yes isn't it lovely?"*

*"There are baby mice nesting under the*
*radiator in your hallway."*

*"Oh did Rosalind give birth already?"*

The Heirloom House

It was always clear to me that there was much more delight than severity in the way Nantucket WASPS shunned material "improvements." These were no Puritans denouncing the vanity of lace collars. One has only to witness the twinkle in the eye of an old codger recalling the "storage" rafters, garden hose plumbing and ladder stairs of his childhood summer home to understand that there was a lot of joy in the pastoral simplicity these summerhouses epitomized. True to its name, a vacation house offered a blissful reprieve from the norms of year-round living—a vacation from entertaining that demanded formal china, furniture that imposed correct posture, and standards of maintenance that required vigilance.

While this pride in "roughing it" on vacation was widespread in America, from at least the end of the nineteenth century to the mid-century of my childhood, Nantucket could certainly claim one of the most charming expressions of it. By the end of the nineteenth century, as tourism began to replace whaling as Nantucket's chief economy, clusters of seventeenth-century fishing shacks, as small as garden sheds, as misshapen as the backs of old horses, became popular summer cottages.

A few of these huts dated back to the days when the Native Americans on this island taught white settlers how to set out from shore in tiny little boats and catch enormous whales offshore. They were one-room structures, built to accommodate a six-man boat crew, but not comfortably. Often a loft was constructed at the sleeping end of the house, accessible by cleats in the wall or a ladder. Loft ceilings were about 3 feet high. Men, not children, slept under the rafters, nestled tightly among spiders and—perhaps more chafing—each other. Being seamen, they were used to packing into berths and sleeping with the wind and rain pounding a few inches from their heads.

Indeed, much of the architecture of those houses was simply Ship Building 101. Like ships, many of the houses had migrated from other fishing areas on the island, or only pieces of houses had migrated when additions

sense anyone who's ever lived in a Manhattan apartment understands.

I had summer friends who vacationed in these real-life equivalents to Badger's house from *The Wind in the Willows*. Many had windows two feet off the ground and roofs that ended at your waist and yards four feet deep, surrounded by

were needed—the advantage of wood frame structures. Sometimes the sea below the bluff coughed up pieces of decking for walls or hatch doors or ornamentation like quarter boards.

Because the hamlet's "founders" were practical men, they had seen the advantage of clustering together to shield each other from wind and rain and loneliness. Their hut lots were small and additions required ingenious departures from architectural conventions. Angling a wing on a diagonal or adding a second story to only one room of the house or putting a bedroom on the street in front of the living room all made the kind of

the trellis if they didn't mind the rose thorns.

The ancient pedigree of these houses made them prime real estate. In the 1960s, lawyers, doctors, and bankers ducked their heads to enter their 12-foot square "Great Room," leading at one end to a 9-foot by 22-foot addition, which usually contained two bedrooms. If you walked down the rutted road that intermittently divided clusters of cottages, you were two feet away from a bed pillow nestling against a window. Curtains made out of embroidered linen napkins were all that was needed for 18-inch windows. Storage space being what it was—or

three-foot tall fences, which you could raise your leg and walk over, never mind the gate. My beloved Rosemary, dearest to me because she was mine, was unquestionably of the house species. She had a front stair with railing and normal finishes like plaster and doorknobs. These fishing cottages had wood plank walls, clanking iron thumb latches, and ladders that led up to sleeping lofts. Better yet, aloft you were still within leaping distance of the ground, should you happen to want a night's adventure, either by defenestration through the porthole at your pillow, or by invitation to friends on the ground who could scale

wasn't—even windows sustained shelves on which you could spy a proud collection of Rockingham mugs, jelly jar glasses, milk glass vases, briar pipes, brass candlesticks stockpiled for outages. Almost one hundred years before my summers in 'Sconset, a US Circuit Court Commissioner named Ansel Judd Northrup wrote a jolly account of the summer in which his family of seven squeezed themselves into one of these cottages: "The cottage, a little one story house with low ceilings and queer little rooms, shingle-sided, and odd in every feature internal and external, was as full as a bee-hive and a vast deal noisier. It was a marvel how we all got into it, and turned around when once in it . . . "

Later in life, I learned the origin of this cluster of houses by reading the work of a nineteenth-century real estate developer, journalist, lawyer, stenographer, and vineyard owner named Edward Underhill. He was so taken with their charm when he vacationed on the island in the early 1880s that he wrote a book about them. And then he built thirty-six copies of them. What I also discovered was that he was an early apostle in the cult of the tattered and threadbare. But you should really hear his whole story, from the beginning. . . .

The Heirloom House

# 2

# Edward Underhill and the Cult of the Tattered & Threadbare

**A**s distinct movements in history are often a serendipitous encounter between social forces and a charismatic leader, at the end of the nineteenth century 'Sconset's little summer cottages found their leader, a man named Edward Underhill. Underhill was a person so constitutionally enthusiastic for projects that within months of his discovery of 'Sconset's "fishing shacks" they became a borderline cult. He had been a stenographer, a journalist, a lawyer, a teacher, a vineyard owner and then, under the spell of Nantucket, he became a developer . . . of fishing shack knock-offs. To me, he also ranks as the founding father of the instant heirloom house.

In 1879 Underhill and his family spent their first summer on Nantucket, in one of 'Sconset's antique cottages. He responded symbiotically to their architectural eccentricities: their unscripted additions; their salvaged

The Heirloom House

components; their playhouse proportions. Within the year he bought a tract of land in the village, carved a dirt road down the center of it and had a local builder, a seventy-something "living relic" named Asa P. Jones, build him a family cottage that looked like it had walked right out of 'Sconset's old fishing hamlet to get a little breathing room. It had taken a little over a fortnight to build and it was named "the China Closet" apparently for two reasons. One reason was that it housed his vast china collection. The other reason is yours to guess.

On the remainder of the plot, he drew plans for two rows of quixotic little cottage cousins to his favorite village shantytown.

Deciding now to commit himself wholeheartedly, not to say, obsessively, he sold a vineyard he owned in Upper New York State and purchased another plot of land adjacent to his first, carved out two more roads, which he named after his

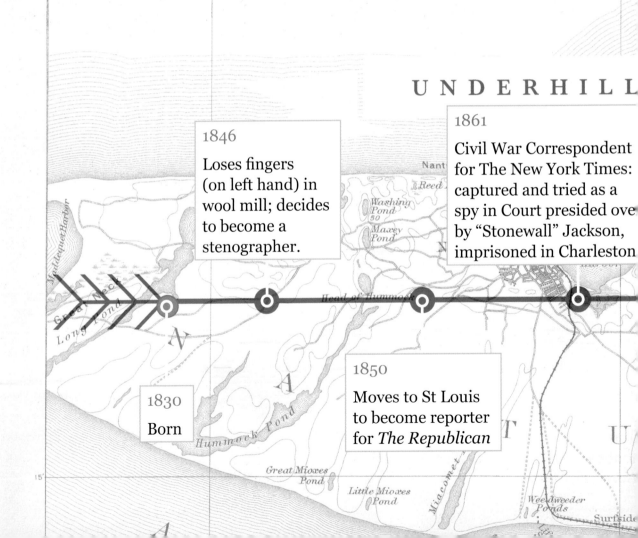

UNDERHILL

**1846**

Loses fingers (on left hand) in wool mill; decides to become a stenographer.

**1861**

Civil War Correspondent for The New York Times: captured and tried as a spy in Court presided ove[r] by "Stonewall" Jackson, imprisoned in Charleston[.]

**1850**

Moves to St Louis to become reporter for *The Republican*

**1830**

Born

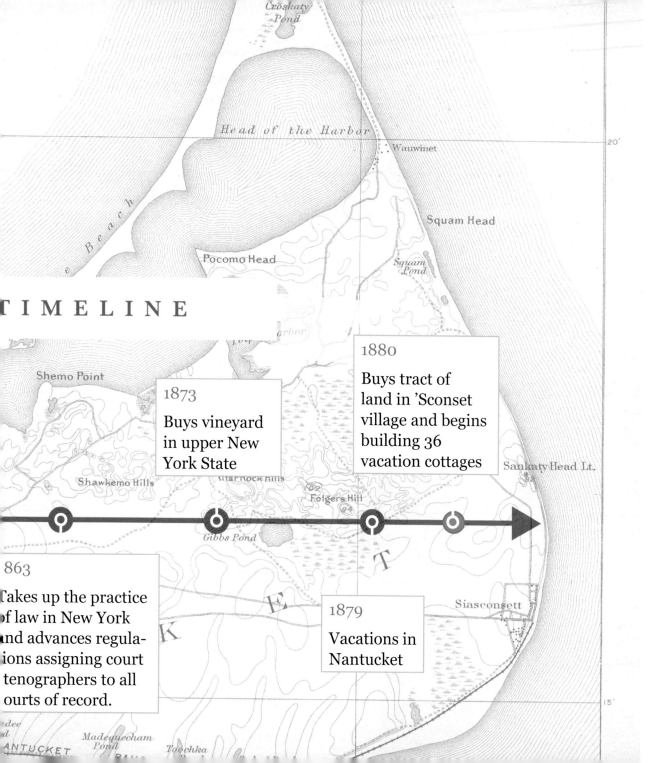

# TIMELINE

**1863**

Takes up the practice of law in New York and advances regulations assigning court stenographers to all courts of record.

**1873**

Buys vineyard in upper New York State

**1879**

Vacations in Nantucket

**1880**

Buys tract of land in 'Sconset village and begins building 36 vacation cottages wife and daughter, Evelyn and Lily, and built what amounted to, when all was done and much said, thirty-six snug little fishing cottage spin-offs. His hunch was that these cottages would become popular and hence lucrative little vacation rentals. His hunch was correct but that suggests a level of passivity uncharacteristic of Underhill, who, though always espousing the somnolence-inducing virtues of Nantucket air, never seems to have rested, not even for a second. Case in point, his "hunch" that his cottages would be popular was reinforced by a one-man PR campaign that puts him neck to neck with Goodby Silverstein, of "Got Milk" fame, in being able to make anything sexy . . . or at least very cool.

What exactly was the allure that Underhill capitalized on? What had Underhill seen in the eighteenth-century shacks that he wanted to replicate?

If you have ever visited Marie Antoinette's hamlet on the grounds of Versailles, you have some idea. In deference to his teenage queen's antipathy for the court, Louis XVI provided her with an escape from its suffocating decorum, its grandeur, and, well, its occupation by him. In her own little hamlet, roofs were thatched, sheep grazed, cabbages and cauliflower grew, and there was a lawn for playing boules like regular folk. The queen could imagine herself a peasant, taking a break from the pomp of her life. This was essentially the wish fulfilled by Underhill's cottages.

Smallness was an asset, both because it allowed vacationers to amuse themselves with ship fantasies and it reduced chores, not the least of which were potential guests. Leaf through 'Sconset albums of the nineteenth century and you will see clusters of people drinking and talking on porches, meeting over fences, gathering at the pump, sitting in groups on front lawns, hanging out at the post office, in other words, having a gay old social time . . . but not in their houses. Just as seven-foot bedrooms are for sleeping only, ten-foot living rooms are for family only. In Underhill's 'Sconset, the burden of formal entertaining is left to the winter months. Isn't that what vacations are for? But should a tenant let his guard down and invite a guest, of course Underhill had devised a way to accommodate the interloper. Taking a cue from his fishing shack forebears, he designed his own migrating addition—a mobile room that could be hauled to any cottage by mule and provide a temporary bedroom when needed. Much better than that cot they put in hotel rooms these days.

That vacation should involve a change of lifestyle was Underhill's key insight and promotional pitch. "The enjoyments of life are heightened by change," he wrote in his typical hybrid of advertising and proselytizing. While a simplified lifestyle might have been the cottages' greatest allure, the cottages offered a leap of the imagination that was an equally essential form of change as far as Underhill was concerned. His cottages made it easy to imagine you were living at sea. There were ladders for stairs, peep holes for windows, and floors that settled into undulations and convex shapes much like ships' cabins. The bedrooms were merely berths, the closets simply lockers. All of these descriptions were included in his advertising. You had the advantage of a seaman's life but without fear of "drifting on land in darkness or in fog, or being driven on a lee shore in gales" he wrote. Another brochure's copy reads: "Inside, little space, big accommodation. Six to nine rooms. Sailors knew how to stow cargo, human livestock or freight."

From our vantage point, it's remarkable that Underhill could afford to make such fun of his cramped cottages. Recently I visited a real estate website where "atrium" was one of the options for narrowing your search. Just try to conceive a world in which Underhill's cottages had online rental search categories: instead of number of bedrooms—berths; instead of family room—porch; hallway—ladder; French doors—portholes; Roche Bobois furnishings—grandma's junk.

Underhill's rental marketing involved quite a bit of cunning. Sometimes his advertisements morphed into travel articles for publication in both regional and national newspapers. And who exactly was writing these travel articles requires a fair amount of detective work as, in the spirit of Benjamin Franklin, Underhill adopted pseudonyms and sometimes created elaborate fictional identities.

*Watertown Post*—September 1884 (p. 25) "The cottages all look as if they were never made by man, but had been by some curious freak pitched together by the sea. Yet inside they are charmingly cozy and snug and filled with wonderful china and stately clocks and rare curiosities from all quarters of the earth. The waves tumble and toss and glitter and roll and rear up greenly and dash down foamingly, and roar and hiss and splash and bubble and chase each other madly and belch forth each other furiously and thunder and dash and play merrily all the while on 'Sconset beach."

Anyone familiar with Underhill's advertising pamphlets should have been suspicious as to how his fictional authors captured his sensibility and style . . . and how zealous they were in their endorsement of his success: "Visitors obviously like the simplicity, liberty and unconventionalism that herein in the place and its traditions, are not satisfied with anything foreign thereto." Very often one particular line gives Underhill's authorship away—in this case a concluding rhetorical flourish. I imagine he rather enjoyed having his cleverness discovered—why else add a line in such signature style, the way a murderer might leave a lace handkerchief or a playing card?

As if all of this construction activity were not enough to fill his summers, Underhill undertook to furnish his little three-lane village himself. Apparently, it mattered as much to him that eccentric eclecticism characterized the house furnishings as it did the houses. What exactly did that mean as a look? It seems he wanted to recreate the sense of generations gathering their found treasures that he so loved to observe in the fishing shacks. His descriptions of the antique oddities found in the ancient fishing shacks exude his relish for them:

> "mirrors of French plate glass and frames of fantastic scroll work; or others of early American manufacture, with the plate surmounted by a landscape painted on glass, showing impossible trees, impractical houses and lakes, the solid waters of which exhibit all the hues of a vigorous but eccentric rainbow; cutlery and crockery of odd shapes and patterns and of all ages . . . and no house is furnished with any thought of the unity of design . . ."

In 1890 a visitor described Underhill's cottage furnishings in much the same way: "Rag carpets such as our great-grandmothers wrought; odd chairs in the fashion of the last century; tables and bedsteads of strange patterns; bureaus with glass knobs or brass handles; clocks of a remote age from Connecticut, England or Holland; fantastic mirrors, violating every principle of art, and other antique things that have recently become the mode again. Old furniture dealers in New York would find here many prizes, but no ordinary sum would buy what has been secured with so much search and trouble" (*I & M*, July 25, 1891).

Before Dorothy Draper and Lady Mendl were furnishing New York hotels and penthouses with shocking combinations of Chinoiserie, animal prints, Victorian tables, and metallic finishes, Underhill was in Nantucket furnishing summer homes with a mixture of rag rugs and Rococo gilded mirrors (minus a few gilds). How he rounded up enough bits and pieces of "shabby chic" and nautical charm to furnish thirty-six cottages inspires the imagination. A poem published in Nantucket in 1898 gives us a clue. It is by Henry S. Wyer, titled "The Relic Auction." Here is an excerpt:

> *"The veteran crier hath been his rounds,*
> *Emitting hoarse, staccato sounds –*
> *Coherent to the natuve ear,*
> *To listening strangers not so clear:*

*"Big Auction on the Lower Square!"*
*And see, the crowd is gathering there;*
*The clock strikes ten in yonder tower,*
*And, prompt upon the appointed hour,*
*The well-known figure, gray and spare,*
*His rostrum mounts – a battered chair!*

*. . . An old man's crutches here you see*
*(A well-known figure once was he) . . .*
*And here's Aunt Debby's coffee mill!*
*Six old Dutch plates—the real Delft'—*
*(Madam, don't bid against yourself);*
*cracked, but good as new;*
*Now, Underhill, a prize for you!*

The number of now coveted "nautical" items listed in other stanzas of the poem: "one compass," "a fine ship's medicine chest," "one whale-oil lamp with can to fill it," "one bull's eye lantern," "one model whaleship on the billows," "one compass, – Walter Folger's make:" gives us a bird's eye view of the material Underhill had to work with.

The fact that two thirds of Nantucket's population had fled the island in the middle of the nineteenth century—a diaspora created by the end of the island's whaling industry—

was an obvious boon to collectors like Underhill. Sam Adams Drake, a travel writer who visited the island in the mid-1870s wrote that the island appeared "uninhabited. Here, indeed was the town, but where were the people? A large proportion of the houses, it would appear, were un-occupied" (*Nooks and Corners of the North East Coast*). Unoccupied houses on an island from which furnishings had to be shipped amounted to a goldmine for the remaining antique-inclined.

The auctioneer's recommendation of four Delft plates to Underhill was a not-too-inside joke. Underhill's original family cottage, the China Closet, had at some point become a tourist attraction. Always an avid collector of antique pottery—platters, plates, pitchers, cups, and saucers—he covered every inch of his cottage's interior with his "finds." Though not quite a museum, it was certainly open to the public for tours and, for the right price, for sales. In August 1897 a brief article appeared in Nantucket's local newspaper reporting that, routinely, eight to ten carriages can be observed visiting the china collection at the China Closet. "the interior has been painted in gray tints, and the brilliant effect of the color of the China is greatly enhanced . . . On Tuesday last he began the illumination of the interior at night, and the display is even more brilliant than in the day."

Underhill included "the China Closet" as a sight "not to be missed" in his advertising circulars. "Visits to the China Closet—a whole house in itself. More than 1,000 pieces of old crockery—Lambet, Staffordshire, Bristol, Newhall, Leeds, Lowestoft, Stoke-upon-Trent, Delft, in place. The work of old potters, Whieldon, Wedgewood, Van Hamme, Davenport, Hancock, Holdship, Alcock, Mayer, Challinor, Copeland, Hall, Enouch Wood (the old deep blue now the craze of collectors), Adams, Clews, Jackson, Minton, Phillips, Riley, Ridgeway, Rose, Stephenson, Spode, Stubbs and others."

(There is more!!!!!!)

"Many views historical—especially those of America; some portraits, some scenic, and some original. Pewter platters, pewter plates, pewter porringers, pewter mugs, pewter spoons, metal teapots. No piece in the collection less than 50; some two hundred years old — a dazzling display on roof boards, rafters, sides and shelves."

Is anyone surprised that a man who built three dozen, no-two-alike cottages would prove to have been a collector as well? After all, he had followed the rule of three (two does not a collection make) and the rule of diversity and, last but not least, the rule of excess.

Sadly, Underhill died suddenly, in New York, at age sixty-eight. But to this day, his cottages have invited their inhabitants to enjoy the playfulness of summer the way he saw it.

The "Underhill cottages" as they were called, became the favorite destination of early film and stage actors who, lured by the low cost, responded also to the warm informality and, well, the fancifulness of it all. In the days before air-conditioning, Broadway shut down for the summer, scattering actors to lakesides or sunny beaches where remoteness was no obstacle, given the luxurious length of their stay. Leave it to actors to make a summer full of lemonade out of their lemon of unemployment.

Within a decade, this frolicking community built themselves a hall of amusement called the "'Sconset Casino" wherein they entertained each other with concerts, dances, skits, and Casey at the Bat style dramatic monologues. And then, as the saying goes, money followed art. One journalist observed that while "Underhill built his cottages with the idea that they would be taken by persons having incomes from $1000 to $3000 . . . their tenants have mainly, to his surprise, been persons with greatly larger incomes." Perhaps not exactly the retreat of a French queen, they seem to have suited plenty of lawyers, bankers and doctors.

In 1965, after three summers renting on the island, my parents signed on with a real estate agent to investigate a summer home purchase. It so happened that one of Underhill's nineteenth-century cottages, "The Doll's House" was on the market. But its $13,000 price tag was a little steep and, while rooms had been added in the course of the twentieth century, the cottage seemed incapable of containing three adolescents. In the end, my parents appear to have had deeper reservations about the wisdom of vacationing at all with teenagers, as, soon thereafter, my brothers were required to find summer employment in our home territory and we ceased to vacation as a family for a good twenty years.

Recently I asked my mother how she survived losing her family vacations. Her answer came without a moment's hesitation: "Jimi Hendrix made it very easy in those days." I imagined "Purple Haze" emerging in stereo from the little portholes and peepholes of The Doll's House and the house rocking in ways that had nothing to do with the sea.

Thus I learned that I had missed,
by perhaps that morning's irritating
burping contest, the chance of
inheriting an old nineteenth-century
summerhouse. As usual my fate
had been tethered, like a sink-line,
to the ignominious behavior of my
brothers. So, after only three years,
our summers in Nantucket ended.
Rosemary's eerie beauty was locked
away in memory, secure from the
tunnel vision of my adolescence and
the realism of my adulthood. She
became a lost Eden—every table doily
and needlepoint footstool, a lost
gardenia and lilac shrub.

Sherry Lefevre

3

*Finding the House*

In 2008, not long after I discovered eBay, a constellation of stars aligned, directing my return to Rosemary. Or rather to my best approximation of her.

Well, yes, first of all I came into an inheritance.

My parents had generously gifted their 1960s summer Rancher to their four children and we failed so miserably at collectively managing it that the house threw roof shingles at our heads and spewed septic at our butts. We sold the house after a few years and my share became the sine qua non of my eBay house project.

But there were other signs as well: 1) fallout from the burst real estate bubble had lowered Nantucket's two-million-dollar floor on summerhouses to . . . well . . . a million-dollar floor. 2) Two other Bright Stars were my children—more like meteors really, shooting farther and farther away from home, threatening to create independent constellations of their own. 3) Another star, bright now but flickering on and off in worrisome ways, was my courage to undertake a major house project. At

fifty-eight, I was still in fighting trim . . . but for how long?

Initially the prospect of shopping for an old house in Nantucket town excited me. I saw it as legitimate trespassing. Truth-be-told, less legitimate trespassing, during the island's deserted winter months, had become my own version of Florida's "stand your ground" law. Mine was more of a "stand their ground," wherein I became a self-appointed caretaker who ensured that beautiful decks overlooking the harbor were holding up. But the houses in town were inviolable, summer and winter. As often as I had walked the brick and cobbled streets, I had only been inside the handful that were museums. From the outside, they all looked like museums and I imagined, foolishly, the time capsules they contained.

It turned out the experience of looking for an old Nantucket house was like getting a bad order of mussels. Shell after empty shell. Who knew that all those nineteenth-century grey-shingled facades no longer contained their naturally sloppy but delicious meat? It was all at the bottom of the pot somewhere, or in this case, the dump. The real estate boom of the 1990s had motivated real estate agents, investment groups, island contractors, heirs and hairdressers, to buy up and gut for resale every antique that came on the market. Almost to a person, their renovations made the same bland assumptions about the target buyer: multi-million-dollar price tags required voluminous living /dining / kitchen areas; marble bathrooms; stone countertops; Poggenpohl cabinets; stainless steel appliances; re-laid and leveled floors; reconstructed walls and pinpoint, recessed lighting. There might still be an old fireplace mantel, removed and then reinstated after walls were torn out to make way for air-conditioning ducts, but the rest of the woodwork is a new and perfect version of the old, as much like it as Brittany Spears is like Marilyn Monroe.

Rosemary had appeared on the Nantucket real estate market the year before. Her floors had been reset and polished, her walls stripped of paper and painted white, her kitchen furbished with uniform cabinets and stainless steel appliances . . . and her price tag was $3,895,000.

"Why does your house have to be old," my real estate agent asked. "You'll save yourself a lot of trouble if you buy a newer one." Her voice lowered an octave mid-sentence indicating she had moved into woman-to-woman mode. We had just looked at three houses that had been built in the last ten years. She'd insisted I humor her by starting with them (all unquestionably very good deals) before becoming too committed to my old house obsession. My blank expression when she pointed out a trash compacter and pantry shelves that extended out and in like an accordion, had prompted this last ditch effort. I was single after all. Relieving myself of a decision to add leaky windows and rotting joists to life's bounty could make a lot of sense. So I thanked her warmly instead of launching into the following self-righteous panegyric on old houses:

"Why did my house have to be old?" It had to be old because of the smell of sunbaked wood in the attic and of musty plaster in the hallways. It had to be old because of the heaving and hoeing that old houses do, that sudden unhinging, window rattling, screen-door slamming melodrama old houses engage in when the mood is on them. It had to be old because the nauseatingly maudlin motto of *The Velveteen Rabbit* is true, more or less: to become real a house needs to show some wear, some shabbiness, some misshapenness, some evidence of love and life within.

I wanted an old house perhaps because I was single, not in spite of it. In an old house, my family would no longer be flotsam and jetsam on the changing sea of me, but rooted in an extended past which gave assurances of an extended future. But mostly I wanted an old house because Rosemary was old and because Rosemary had fixed connotation in the way only childhood experiences do, hard and fast, like the pistons on an engine that has seized.

It took two and a half years to find a house that met the Goldilocks test—not too big, not too small, not too derelict, not too gussied up, not too close to the town center, not too far, just a nice, unremarkable old house (that I could afford). The listing gave its date of origin as 1865, but it seemed older than that. Like most of Nantucket's nineteenth-century houses it was basically a square wooden box with a chimney running through the middle. The front living room, side dining room and side back parlor pivoted on this central chimney with fireplaces drawing to the same stack. It had the usual shed kitchen. There were a couple of other "warts" as Nantucketers call them. In the back, a mini-shed had been added to create a bathroom. Off the front hall, opposite the living room, there was a one-story room with a pitched ceiling, probably an act of salvage from another dwelling. It was being used as a laundry room (with a desk in it), but I could imagine a guest room there. Steep basement stairs led to a circular brick root cellar, and alarmingly precipitous wooden stairs climbed up the mortar of the chimney to the attic. The door opening to these attic stairs was in a back bedroom on the second floor. It was the last stop on my real estate agent guided tour. I clicked open its thumb latch; stared at the raw wood ladder-like stair, and thought, *I will buy this house*. Why? Because it met the Goldilocks test and it was as real as a furless rabbit and those back attic stairs reminded me of Rosemary. Also . . . I could afford it.

*

Like most house buyers, it was only after I was contractually committed to ownership that I began to get to know my house. Home ownership is what I imagine arranged marriages to be like. You've barely met and then you wake up one morning, staring at a wall that is yours in perpetuity.

Your pre-marital meetings were supervised, chaperoned as it were, by real estate agents. (My pre-marital house courtship had lasted all of fifteen minutes.) You felt sheepish about opening closets or looking behind the shed in the backyard. All told, it's a fairly blind, good faith commitment.

Since I actually have a great deal of respect for arranged marriages, I find the analogy comforting. By far the majority of the arranged marriages I have known have worked out very well. They are carefully, lovingly orchestrated unions between people with shared values. Not surprisingly, when people have mutual standards of right conduct, deeply ingrained by their culture, they grow into love for each other. So too homeowners and their houses. But it takes work, and patience, for initial attraction to become something deeper.

Phase one of my relationship with the new house was purely physical. I touched every inch of it with my hands and then with spackle, sandpaper, wood putty, primer and paint. Seven days a week for two months.

I learned to paint houses from someone who loved walls the way others love horses, and greeted them with those same tender strokes of her hand. When I first met her, she was considering a job painting my old house in Philadelphia. I had exhausted myself stripping wallpaper that had frescoed onto plaster walls with a tenacity unequalled in my experience. After the usual hello, she leaned into the wall I'd been working on, her cheek almost grazing it and rubbed it back and forth with her

hand. "Can't you just hear it sighing—like a man whose balls haven't been rubbed for a long time?" she said. She died from lung cancer, a devastating occupational hazard, and I miss her and I try to honor her in the smoothness of my walls. Also, in my appreciation of how an untended house needs stroking.

My next step was to learn what the house could tell me about its life before me. This impulse stems, I think, from respect as much as curiosity. Pleased as I am to take possession of this house, I also recognize that houses, like people, exist independently and are shared by others, past and future. Like any artifact from the past . . . like most of what I bought on eBay, a house often contains in microcosm, the historical narrative of its time and place. For those of us who found history textbooks overwhelming, it's a relief to have such a tangible, diminutive, visual prompt for historical memory. Nantucket's narrative is a particularly interesting one so I felt privileged to own a house

that was part of it, albeit something of a walk-on.

This is probably the right place to take a brief detour into Nantucket's history.

Here's a Brothers Grimm version:

*For one hundred years, a whaling empire ruled this tiny patch of land. From the middle of the eighteenth century to the middle of the nineteenth century, fleets of Nantucket owned ships set sail from Nantucket's harbor for the often uncharted waters of the Southern Atlantic and the Pacific. Nantucket's indigenous Native American population had shown the white settlers how to fish for whales off the eastern shore. After discovering the enhanced value of the sperm whale, the settlers set sail in tall ships for distant seas, their voyages taking as long as four years. Soon enough, the islanders had created a whole industry out of the pursuit of this sea monster.*

*By the beginning of the nineteenth century, the success of Nantucket whalers drew a population of more than ten thousand to the fourteen-mile-long island, making Nantucket the fourth largest town in Massachusetts. At home islanders were employed in refining, marketing and shipping the oil, as well as all manner of preparation required for the ships' long voyages. Their precious commodity fueled the lamps of New England and Europe and their profits*

*built a beautiful town surrounding a busy harbor.*

*Ascending a steep hill above the port were the seaman's houses. From roof balconies they could observe the forest of ship masts below and the stealth of new arrivals sliding through the harbor's narrow channel. The grey and white houses had proud chimneys and deeply paneled doors with transoms and colonnades. Golden church spires gleamed above the hill's crest. A handsome brick bank, with pillared portico, squared off the highest point of the commercial district and captain's houses with sterling silver doorknockers and cupolas, and rooftop observatories lined a cobbled main street.*

*Other shipping magnates built houses that extended every inch of themselves along the harbor town's highest ridge, like turkeys showing off plumage in a mating dance.*

*Then the magic ended. Within a single decade a series of events conspired, like evil spells, to cripple the town. By 1840 the harbor had silted over so grievously, ships couldn't approach the docks; in 1846 the docks burned and along with them one third of the town; and in 1848 the discovery of gold at Sutter's Mill operated like the Pied Piper, drawing Nantucket's frustrated younger generation westward, emptying the town. In 1852 kerosene was refined from petroleum, and became a cheaper, more plentiful substitute for whale oil. If not a fairy tale's curse, certainly a lesson in the risks of a non-diversified economy. Within three decades, two thirds of the island's population had abandoned it. Time in the wood shingled and clapboard town, stood still.*

From the point of view of someone interested in historic preservation, this might be the best thing that could happen to a town. The abrupt end of Nantucket's glittering heyday operated like volcanic ash, locking the historic moment, petrifying it. Had life continued as usual, Victorian houses would have replaced Federal, then Italianate and Renaissance Revival might have claimed the captains' majestic views, and later who's to say that Prairie style might not have crouched down along the entrance to the harbor before succumbing to early-modern and then postmodern geometry.

Not that there's anything wrong with that.

Unless you particularly like very old houses. Which, of course, I do.

I was right that my house was older than 1865. My first endorsement

came from David, an architect who serves on the island's architectural review board. He lives down the street and came over for a visit. Two steps into the house, he asked to feel my rafters. I guess old houses

just bring out the lascivious in people. I led him to the magical attic stair. He ascended into the pitch black while I stood at the open door, listening to his mental backwash: "no ridge beam" "uhaa" "interesting" "I'm trying to feel … well not protruding … " I felt like I was undergoing a breast exam, waiting for the doctor to finally remember that my eyes and ears were stuck to the top of what he was looking at.

He reemerged, gingerly. "Definitely not 1865."

Apparently he had found the trunnels (6-inch wooden pins driven into the rafters) he was groping for. (Trunnel is a word born sometime in the eighteenth century and it appears to be short for tree nail).

After casing the rest of the joint, he assembled this list of telltale indicators of the house's early nineteenth-century origin.

1   There was a mirror board in the living room. Who knew that the fat piece of wooden paneling above the

chair rail, and between my two front windows, was not a piece of molding someone forgot to take off when they re-plastered? Sitting on the wall across from the fire, it was where a mirror should go, and it protected the wall from the mirror's lower edge. This also explained the smaller, flat board at the ceiling edge above it, called a picture rail. It allowed the mirror's hook to be anchored.

2   The window muntins were exceedingly narrow. Indeed, compared to Andersen windows, they look like sticks.

3   The glass in the windows is neither float glass, as it would be in later houses, nor bull's-eye (or Crown glass), as it would be in earlier houses. It is cylinder glass. Float glass is made by floating molten glass on lead until it cools, creating a perfect, flat surface. bull's-eye panes are made by spinning molten glass at the end of a rod, as you would do to pizza dough. This extended glass disc is cut into panes. Cylinder glass is made by blowing a blob of glass into a large cylindrical tube, cutting the ends, slitting the tube down one side and placing this in a special oven where it will unfold and flatten. Both Bull's Eye panes and Cylinder panes contain ripples, especially visible when you move back and forth on your vantage point. But what distinguishes them is the shape of these ripples. My Cylinder panes have linear ripples. Bull's Eyes have curved ripples. If you don't know why, reread the last paragraph.

The Heirloom House

4   The hardware or ironmongery in the house is hand wrought. Later door handles were machine made. Earlier doors had wooden levers.

5   The profiles of the doors, windows and fireplaces are pre-Federal period. Most of us would call this the molding. For these to be "profiles" you have to line yourself with the wall (which is something I'm not used to doing) and see how the wood trim is shaped and stacked. Apparently later profiles have more ellipses and ovals and bullnoses. My fireplace surrounds are faced with flat recessed panels and the mantel itself sits on a series of thin, graduated planks of wood—no rounded edges until the top and bottom transitional pieces. There are more stacked pieces on the living room mantel than in the dining room and back parlors. Just goes to show who's king of rooms.

"Case closed," I concluded, "early nineteenth century."

David was shaking his head. "Well . . ."

There was that high pitch in his voice that comes from the truth trying to squeeze through too tight a pigeonhole. The problem, I was about to learn, is that early Nantucket architecture was always somewhat retro. Stylistic trends and new building methods seem to have hit "irons" crossing the Sound. Or perhaps Island craftsmen were simply truculent, set in their ways, and less harassed by clients needing to be style setters.

Whatever the reason, a Nantucket house often appears to be twenty or even fifty years older than it actually is. Its architectural detail may simply be a holdover from an earlier time. Everything David had pointed out might indicate only how structurally odd my house was.

## 4
## Getting to Know My House

So off to the Office of Deeds and Records, I went. Tracking old house deeds is apparently as common a pastime on Nantucket as scalloping and birding. No one in the Deeds office even looks up when you make your inquiry; they look at each other and whoever blinks first gets up and heads to the computer. But the computer will only take you backwards to the late nineteenth century. After that the task becomes more arduous. Earlier deeds of title transfer are handwritten in huge bound portfolios, which are beautiful but heavy.

I was graced with a clerk named Jessica, who immediately warmed to the task and then became my own Ferdinand Magellan. There was a particularly narrow strait where the house moved sideways between owners rather than backwards. But she stayed the course and finally we anchored on a deed where only land was being transferred—no dwelling. That was 1819. The house was about forty-five years older than what had been recorded by the assessor. Of course it was. That meant that it was built at about the time of Rosemary (1820). But why was the assessor so far off? Hmmm. The last computer-generated deed was 1865. Someone didn't want to lug those beam-like volumes around.

The deeds tell you the names of your house ancestors. Armed with those names, you can go to the Eliza Starbuck Barney genealogical record and watch your tiny piece of information spread like ink on a damp matte board.

In 1819 Walter Cure purchased the deed for my land and then in 1825 sold the deed for my land and a "dwelling house thereon". So we can assume he built the house himself or hired a builder. The rest of his family genealogy suggests he might have been in a hurry. From the genealogical records we see that in the year of his land purchase, his fourth child, John, was born. He and his wife, Lucretia Allen, had child number one, Josiah in 1813. Then came Charles in 1814, Mary in 1816, and John in 1819—four children ages six and under when he bought my lot to build on! Lucretia's brother, Josiah, died at sea in 1804. So she named her first born after him? Sweet.

The records of only two of the four Cure children extend to their deaths; both died off island in the 1870s—Josiah in New York and Mary in Jersey City.

Remember that the end of Nantucket's whaling industry, mid-century, created a population exodus of such magnitude that, by 1875, two thirds of its peak 1842 population of more than 10,000 had left. Josiah and Mary Cure were presumably in that exodus.

The rise and fall of the house's sale price tells the same story of Nantucket's economic rise and decline in the nineteenth century. In 1819, John Chase sold a "fish lot" share (a term used for these plots of land) to Walter Cure, for $76.80. In 1825, Walter Cure sold the same property on which he built a house to Samuel Robbins for $750.00. In 1848, The Robbins' heirs sold the house to Mary C. Gardner for $500 dollars. And in 1865, when William C. Folger, 3rd. bought the house, he paid only $200. Why did Samuel Robbins pay more for the house in 1825 than his wife's heirs got for it in 1848? Why did William Folger, in 1865, pay half as much as Mary Gardner? Simply put, the only title transfer that occurred during Nantucket's Golden Age of Whaling was Samuel Robbins's.

When Walter and Lucretia's first child was born, and he was in his twenties, the United States was at war with Great Britain. The War of 1812 played havoc with Nantucket's economy in much the way the Revolutionary War had done. At the dawn of war, most of the island's population was engaged in the whaling industry, in one way or another. But immediately after war broke out, whale ships were captured, crews were made prisoners of war, and cargo was destroyed. Not only did the war cost the Islanders their principal source of income, but British ships trawling the shores along the Cape made the waters too dangerous for transport of critical imports from the mainland—corn, grain and wood. Many islanders became destitute. Obed Macy, in his 1835 History of Nantucket, describes, with great compassion, the conditions of life on Nantucket during the war years:

"In a few months after the war commenced, many of the inhabitants were reduced to great distress. Want of employment, as has already been stated, had before reduced large numbers of the laboring class to want; loss of property, and other circumstances was now bringing others to poverty. It was difficult to procure flour and corn . . . Hundreds of the laboring poor might daily be seen in the streets, destitute of the means to subsistence, because destitute of employment . . . Removals from the island still continued, some to avoid present distress, others with a view to permanency [sic]."

Walter Cure was not one of those who "removed" himself from the island; his children were born in quick succession in Nantucket, beginning in 1813. On the other hand, there is no record of his owning property prior to purchasing land for my house in 1819. Given the conditions on the island before then, this is not surprising.

When the war ended in 1814, Nantucket's whaling fleet had been reduced by half, to twenty-three ships. But by 1819, the year of Cure's land purchase, the whaling fleet was a healthy sixty-one. In characteristic fashion, Islanders had jumped back into whaling with a vengeance. The year 1819 was also the year the famous whaling ship *Essex* set sail from Nantucket, bound for the Pacific Ocean. Three months into their voyage they were rammed and rammed again by an eighty-five-foot long, very angry, Spermaceti whale. Melville would later call the whale Moby Dick and spin his own yarn. In reality, the whale shattered the *Essex*, dispersed the crew, and thence began a tale of even greater horror when scant provisions induced cannibalism in one of the lifeboats. Yes, while that was going on, Walter Cure was busy erecting a dwelling on Pine Street.

My house was never owned by a ship captain, like so many of the houses surrounding me. I don't know what Walter Cure did for a living, but he is not in any of the ship records. Samuel Robbins, who purchased the house from Walter Cure in 1825, was a seaman. Though never a captain, he made it to the rank of First Mate before he died at sea. Perhaps if he had not died at thirty-five, he would have moved up to Captain. Samuel Robbins's name appears on the "Shipping Paper," or contract, for a whaling ship named *Lydia* in 1817. He was Second Mate with a forty-three share. The contract describes the voyage as "To the coast of Brazil and elsewhere." And yet Robbins still signed. Other records indicate that it returned from Brazil and elsewhere in 1818 with 665 bbls of whale oil, hardly enough to pay expenses.

A ship ledger shows that Zenas Coffin, the ship's owner, paid Samuel Robbins 103.00 lay. Let's hope that wasn't his only income for the year. At least he had a few more years to save up for the purchase of my house. Presumably he continued to plumb the seas for whales.

In 1829, four years after buying my house, Samuel set sail as First Mate on the ship *Fabius*, whose captain was Thaddeus Coffin. Its whaling ground was the Pacific Ocean and it returned in 1833, after almost four years at sea, with 2162 barrels of sperm oil. Sadly, Samuel Robbins did not live to enjoy his share. Starbuck's *History of Nantucket* includes a registry of his death on the voyage. "First mate,

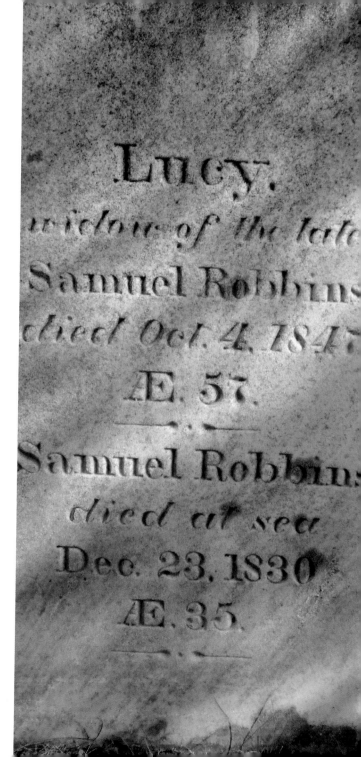

Samuel Robbins died, November 1830." His wife, Lucy survived him by seventeen years. Her grave is in the North Cemetery, and her tombstone can be seen on page 53.

Lucy Robbins died in 1846, the year of the Great Fire. It began in a hat store during a summer dry spell, and spread with a hellish fury through the timber buildings surrounding Main Street. Then it moved to the docks, consuming warehouses filled to the rafters with whale oil. From these warehouses, burning oil poured onto the wharfs and into the harbor, creating a sea of fire. It must have looked like a biblical act of vengeance. God was on the whales' side. One third of Nantucket Town was destroyed. While the fire didn't single-handedly cause Nantucket's economic decline, it handicapped the shipping port at a time when New Bedford was already gaining an edge. Thus Lucy Robbins's heirs sold the Pine Street house in a declining economy.

Only Nantucket's genealogical records contain information on Mary F. Gardner, the next Pine Street owner.

She was born Mary Shute in 1820 and later married Richard Gardner. There is no record of children. Gardners had been around since the seventeeth century but both Mary and Richard Gardner died off island in the 1860s.

The Folger family, a representative of whom was the next owner of my house, is famous beyond Nantucket for having spawned Benjamin Franklin. His mother, Abiah Folger, was the daughter of an early Nantucket settler from England, named Peter. Abiah Folger was born in Nantucket in 1667, married Josiah Franklin and gave birth to Benjamin in 1706. Though my house's owner was a century and a half removed from the most famous family member, my house vanity was briefly teased by uncovering a nineteenth-century Folger of some repute, named William Folger, like my home's owner. He was nineteenth-century Nantucket's foremost genealogist. Indeed, I probably have him to thank for much of my information on my home's early owners. Not only was he a dedicated researcher and recorder, but he had a sweet, untutored drawing style that resulted in a beautiful study of birds when he was a child. The Nantucket Historical Association even has a photo of William C. Folger sitting on the front steps of a house that looks very much like mine. But alas, he was sitting on the steps of his house on Fair, not Pine Street. He was not the William Folger who owned my house.

A William Folger (b. 1828) who might have owned my house was a whaler on the *Monticello*. Of course, his older brother, John Folger, was the captain, not he. He seems to have made several Pacific journeys but after a particularly long one (1853–1858) the ship was sold to a Connecticut owner and thereafter sailed out of New London. Its exile from Nantucket turns out to have been only a minor episode in the *Monticello*'s declining fortunes.

PHOTO CREDIT: NATIONAL HISTORICAL ASSOCIATION

After only four voyages, the *Monticello* was destroyed along with thirty-two other whaling ships when in 1871 the fleet became trapped in arctic ice near Alaska. The 1,219 men on board were forced to abandon ship not only because they could no longer conduct business, but because their ships were crushed by the ice. Miraculously all survived. After crossing more than seventy miles of sea, they were rescued by five whaling ships that had escaped the ice. To bring them on board, the whalers had to unload their precious whale oil cargo adding to a total loss of more than $1,600,000. So Nantucket's Great Fire and arctic ice both played decisive roles in the demise of the industry. If not the world, the world of whaling ended in both Fire and Ice.

Did William Folger read about the fate of his late ship while sitting by the hearth in my house? Was this house his to settle into after years at sea, its warm southern light in the upstairs bedroom a sweet reward? All I'm sure of is that the William Folger who owned my house bought it for half of what the previous owner had paid. He got a real bargain. I can't help but feel some kinship with someone who bought the house when the whole island was at "estate sale" prices.

One afternoon in late October, I rode my bike to the North Cemetery to take a picture of Lucy Robbins's tombstone. The day was filled with the stirrings of winter. A week earlier, the temperature had dropped ten degrees, which cleared the air of mist and gave the sky, the stone wall, the white markers, a hard clarity. The cemetery's few wind-hammered trees cast frantic shadows, making me doubt I would get a clear shot. It was still fall, but I could feel winter in the ground when I kneeled to frame the Robbins's inscription in my viewfinder.

We associate cemeteries with fall, but why? We expect to hear the rustle of dead leaves on gravestones and see racing clouds in a darkening sky, over a full moon. Logically we should associate graveyards with winter—the dead season with the dead. But to the living, like me on my bike, the movement towards death is the only thing we really know about death. Fall is us. Fall is where I stand, looking at Lucy Robbins's grave, two chapters in the same house.

# 5
# *Interior Decorating as the Power of Association*

**B**ecause I teach at a university, it made sense for me to take advantage of the summer of 2009 to furnish my house before I actually owned it. My closing was in September. I needed the house to be rentable by the following Spring. My plan was that on the weekend of my September closing, I would drive a UHaul truck filled with furniture up Route 95 to a freight ferry in Hyannis. As usual, what seemed a perfectly sensible plan to me was, by most reckonings, quite insane. I would be 370 miles away from the house I didn't even own, while I furnished it. I would be buying every lamp, doorstop, faucet, painting, rug, wastebasket I needed before the house had been refurbished by a carpenter and painted by me. And while it would have been nice to have a floor plan of the house, I did not . . . or to be CAD adept, I was not. Nope. But I had a much more powerful tool than either of these. And no, I don't mean love, though my love was true. I had uncanny house memory.

For years, I had been observing and remembering the way people furnished their houses. Thus I became like a "magic sponge" when it hits a basin of water. Presto, my house knowledge went into full and instant bloom as soon as I clicked on eBay. eBay is made for memory sponges like me. Because eBay allows you to "subject index" your memories. You can create a list of the things you want to find—wastebaskets adorned with old lithographs for example—and simply type them into the magic machine.

On eBay, the world of heirloom junk and treasures is indexed and instantaneously retrievable! For an academic with a house to furnish, it was the heirloom equivalent to Harvard's Widener Library.

I clicked to begin my searches on July 7 and by Labor Day I had the vintage/antique furnishings of a four-bedroom Nantucket house—in my Philadelphia hallway. They were also waiting in garages along the Route 95 corridor between Philadelphia and Hyannis, Massachusetts.

I've never hired an interior decorator but I know that they try to understand a client's needs and wants by asking questions like: When you entertain, is it usually just another couple or do you prefer cocktail parties with canapés for legions of attractive acquaintances? I also know that recently ethnographers have jumped into the design arena and insist that the truth of behavior can only be gleaned from observation rather than questionnaire or interview, presumably because, what? People lie? Well, sort of.

So ideally a designer should enter a client's house masquerading as a friend and observe the real truth, which is that the last time you entertained was three years ago when your third cousin from Hawaii emailed from a nearby Comfort Inn and insisted on dropping by.

For what it's worth, I think both designers are barking up the wrong tree. What difference does it make what you think you do or what you really do in a house?

It's what you fantasize that matters.

Is that porch swing there because swinging is the homeowner's favorite pastime? Is that grandfather clock ticking away in a corner because Uncle Roscoe needs to check when the game starts? Is that wall of bookshelves in the living room there to make research convenient? Homeowners know that porch swings, melodious clocks, shelves of books whisper to us when we pass them, saying "I offer you a vicarious life, never demanding that you actually live it. For that reason, you love me." Opening the front door, briefcase in one hand, groceries in another, we glance over our shoulder at the swing gently waving at us—the slightest tremor—and suddenly the image of Ashley coming home from the Civil War, of beautiful Melanie, as pure as buttermilk, leaping up from the swing and running to him, lifts our gait and we enter blithely into the kitchen, dump our groceries and turn on the Nightly Business Report.

I wanted a house full of heirlooms because I wanted to feel layers of life at every turn. I imagined my house as a sort of historical commune where all the people who might have lived within … and their friends, would feel perfectly at home. Nothing I bought would actually be authentic to the house, nor would I attempt to be true to its architectural period. The last thing I wanted was to live in a museum exhibit. Like an equal opportunity employer, I preferred to see antiques of all ages as competing, without prejudice, for a place in my house. Then I would try to create a happy diversity of style and era and at the same time uphold a standard of merit. As it turned out, I did discover that certain periods were better at designing certain objects (in my humble opinion) but no period was so utterly depraved as to offer nothing of interest.

So you could say I had a philosophy, or maybe just a policy, but I still didn't have a plan. A plan might inhibit my urge to drive a shovel truck through the refuse of the past and dump it all in my house.

*The Mission Period delivered up the best bookshelves,*

*the Victorians the most fabulous shell art,*

*the early nineteenth-century, terrific plank-seat chairs,*

*the Edwardian era, the most stunning lamps . . .*

# Creating a Mind Map

I decided to focus on two key words—
Nantucket and Summer—and create
a mind map of the associations those
words generated. My associations
would be the starting point for eBay
"searches."

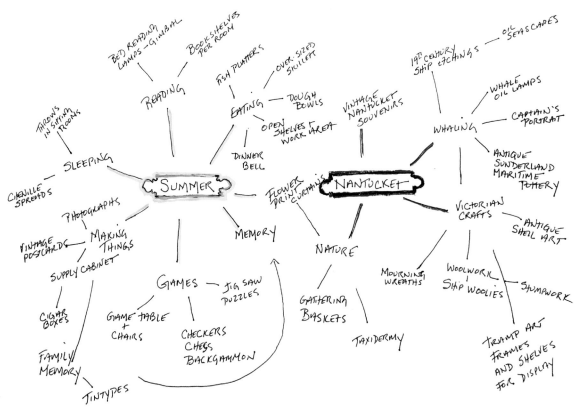

# Summer Associations

As you can see, for me, summer means reading (bookshelves); games (chess, checkers, backgammon, game table and chairs); sleeping (white chenille bedspreads, wool blankets, lots of throws); eating (heavy, jelly-jar type glasses, oversized skillets, fish platters, candles); crafts (making memory objects out of shells and postcards and photographs); while Nantucket means ships and sailing (old seascapes, nautical prints, ship dioramas); whaling (whale oil lamps, whale carvings); shell crafts (sailor's valentines, Victorian shell boxes); vintage Nantucket souvenirs.

Of course, everyone's mind-map for these two concepts would be different. Some people associate summer with gardening or bird watching or fishing or golfing or surfing . . . and their links to household furnishings might include collections of antique fish decoys, Audubon bird prints, antique garden tools, gathering baskets, old seed sacks, Eames era surfboard coffee tables, Hickory golf clubs, art deco golfers lamps . . .

The charm of eBay is that it doesn't require that you solidify your free associations . . . at least not right away. You can enter any of them into your "Search". If you want to create a house with history, you qualify your search terms with words like "antique" or "vintage" or "old" or "19c" or era designations like "Victorian" or "Georgian" and then see what treasures others have associated with that word. Gradually you will learn more precise ways to find what you want, because, well, you figure out what you want.

Here's an example of a rather abstract search I did.

I enter "antique gardening" as my search. I see that there are more than 3,000 listings, so I need to learn how to focus quickly. The third item I come to is a corn planter from 1893. Only one person has bid on it ($14.99) with an hour to go. It is a very cool looking tool with a long wooden handle, original red paint, and it works!!!!!

Do I want to collect corn planters? Hmmm.

Nantucketers did grow corn. Scrolling further, I notice another antique corn planter—looks just like the first one and six people are bidding on it with nine hours to go! Why? Because "farm tool" was added to the subject heading.

*I have already learned two critical points:*

*First*, I can glean productive search categories from scrolling through listings. "Antique farm tool" is a search category that yields a more manageable list of 321 items, almost all of which are interesting. (For instance, the fifth item

under "antique farm tool" is an "antique corn sheller grinder." OMG. I could have a set.)

*Second*, equally important is not to use conventional categories all the time. Had I begun by searching only "antique farm tool," I might miss a corn planter that has escaped general notice because the listing wasn't refined.

*Conclusion:*

Once I've focused on what I want to purchase, I should try lots of "search routes" to get there.

# Nantucket Associations

The same subjectivity that applies to Summer applies to the local vernacular, in this case Nantucket associations. While it's true that the whaling era has captivated the historical imagination of most Nantucket homeowners, there are those who care more about early twentieth-century sailboats; others who dream they are keepers of old lighthouses; more still who cherish the native craft of basket-weaving. Even the meaning of the whaling era is individually nuanced, depending on how much stomach you have for blood and blubber. Some still see it for what it was, and they might choose to hang a whaler's harpoon over their mantel and collect old engravings of arctic expeditions where dying whales lie in the foreground, bleeding to death on icebergs. Other contemporary Island dwellers prefer to stay one step removed, like the house-bound families of whalers. Indeed, the objects that have become iconic of this era show how skillfully we have tilted the glass away from blood and blubber. The most cherished (and valuable) relics

are handicrafts the whalers made for their loved ones back home. We've created chivalrous heroes, focusing on the whaler's manliness (as seen in portraits); his bravery (as seen in tempestuous seascapes and images of whales upending tiny whaleboats); and his fidelity to his island loved ones (every form of seamen's gifts, either purchased or hand-crafted, such as sailor's valentines and scrimshaw). Whaling is the real-life equivalent to dragon slaying.

Of course, whales were not like mythical dragons at all. None that I know of ever attacked a whaler unprovoked and certainly none stole any of our princesses. For this reason, I was never tempted to purchase a whale weapon, though I have seen them on eBay. But a whale oil lamp? Sure. A figurehead from a whaleship? Sure. An etching of a whaler? You bet, as long as it doesn't include the harpooning of a whale. One hundred and fifty years after the fact, whaling is outlawed and excoriated and still remembered with a racing pulse . . . even by whale lovers like me.

My summer associations, I realized, shared a central theme with my Nantucket associations—"downtime." This would be where my two circles overlapped in a Ven diagram. Unlike the rest of the year, summer gives you empty hours to fill, like huge glass bowls or large blank tablets that say, "Make something of me." Being too often cerebral in my work-a-day life, I tend to fill these hours by making something with my hands. So I associate summer with handcrafts of all sorts.

"Downtime" also describes a substantial portion of a whaler's life, and he seems to have had the same impulse to do something with his hands, though to much better effect. Think about it. In between bouts of manning the boats and taking what was called a Nantucket sleigh-ride at the end of a speeding and careening harpoon's line, the crew waited. They sailed around Cape Horn and into the Pacific, sometimes as far north as China. The average length of a whaling voyage in 1840 to 1844 was 43.4 months—

almost four years (compared to 13.7 months in 1804). As the voyages became increasingly long, there was, not surprisingly, a marked increase in decorated scrimshaw. Most of the elaborate scrimshaw you can see in Nantucket's Whaling Museum comes from that period. Ship embroideries, or woolies, experienced a similar impetus. So too the few sailor's valentines actually made by sailors and not purchased by sailors visiting Barbados.

Back home their women also had some downtime. They were on an island after all, with not a rocking social life and no man to wait on hand and foot. So they embroidered, quilted, hooked, crocheted, knitted, knotted (either yarn, or human hair), smocked, beaded, cross-stitched . . . you name it, if you could do it with a needle, they did it. While the craftsmanship on some of these antique objects gives them fine arts status, many handcrafts are considered "folk art" and that is how they are listed on eBay.

I recommend that you enter "antique folk art" as a "search" and feast your eyes. Sure enough, you will find some objects that look like they were done by an antique version of me while on summer vacation.

But you can skip over these and find many examples of a more skillful (if not necessarily happier) use of downtime. This "search" is how I found many of the random treasures that live in my Nantucket house.

Their folk art nature keeps them from being intimidating and the last thing a person wants to be when on vacation is intimidated. They speak, everyman to everyman, urging us along in our creative fantasies. Most of them are also made from scraps of materials readily available. Cigar boxes usually provide the base and the wood for gouging decoration in tramp art. Cigar boxes are also used in shell art, though more frequently shell art makes use of cardboard boxes, painted or covered in decorative paper.

# Treatise on the Borderline Ugly

Inevitably, collecting folk art leads to the philosophical question: What is too ugly? And to me the less obvious but necessary correlative: What is too pretty?

Almost every whaling and nautical artifact in the Nantucket Whaling Museum is either pretty or beautiful. They adhere to classic design principles: symmetry and centralized focus. There are clear hierarchies within each design and enough negative space to maintain a decorous calm. Don't get me wrong; I love them, especially where they sit, in glass and walnut cases, with very gentle illumination so their dyes won't fade. When they sit in summerhouses, on mantels and sideboards, their lifelessness stands out like taxidermy against the happy energy of our lives.

They may suit the temperament of our year-round professional lives but their perfection is not in keeping with the invitation to amateurism that is the key to a good vacation. My own painted scallop shells should not have to stand up against the impeccable designs on a scrimshaw yarn winder.

I bought some "antique folk art apple head dolls" for $14 on eBay. They arrived when my daughter was at home, which was great, since my memory of trying to make apple head dolls with her, years ago, prompted my purchase. Our apple heads turned into lumps of green mold. These dolls looked like they'd come out better. Not, apparently, if you ask my daughter. When I lifted them from

tl.. , she screamed and ran out of the room. She was twenty at the time. So are they too ugly—with their shriveled, shrunken black heads and train-car green dresses? If I told you that nineteenth-century Nantucket girls made apple head dolls would that redeem them?

In 1756 Edmund Burke wrote *A Philosophical Enquiry into the Origin of Our Ideas of the Sublime and Beautiful* in which he demonstrated (among other things) that beauty was not all it was trumped up to be, if you gave the matter any philosophical thought, as he obviously did. According to Burke, our response to subjects that are beautiful involves love and an impulse to touch and possess. Pshaw. Good as that might sound, it doesn't match the nobler sentiments inspired by something greater than beauty, something he calls "sublime" but which I call "borderline ugly."

Apparently our response to sublime subjects, like Rubens's paintings, the Alps, lions, Beethoven's 8th symphony, to name a few, involves fear and awe. And because fear and awe lead directly to thoughts of God and The Eternal (stay with me) they are nobler sentiments. We experience fear and awe when we view the craggy peaks of Mt. Blanc. It is so enormous (and we are so small), its creation so far exceeds our powers (we are so weak), one can't but think of eternity. This too, applies to borderline ugliness.

Take these two shell art boxes I bought on eBay. They are both borderline ugly. But aren't you in awe of them? Don't you kind of fear them? While we might want to caress, even place on our bedside table, an antique lusterware teacup, it will never remind us of how much lies beyond our reach, or how close genius is to madness!

Sherry Lefevre

# 6

# Creating a Budget and the Economics of eBay

**My List of Averages for item types:**

# BENCH MARKS

| | | | |
|---|---|---|---|
| Lamps | $50 | oil paintings | $150 |
| side tables | $100 | prints/small art | $50 |
| old rugs | $200 | wool throws | $30 |
| bureaus | $250 | hanging shelves | $50 |
| beds | $200 | bookshelves | $100 |
| curtains | $400 | shell art | $35 |
| dioramas | $15 | Taxidermy | $35 |

The second step in planning my eBay searches was the equivalent of throwing a bucket of cold water all over my Ven diagrams—in other words, I created a budget. More or less. If you're like me, and you've spent your whole closet life accumulating information about things like what makes palissy majolica (with its linguini-like grass and its fat clay toads) cooler than any other majolica, then an opportunity to furnish an entire house can result in the kind of gluttonous behavior that killed King Henry VIII.

I needed the cold water of a budget.

I employed a method I'd been using for years. I looked at my bank balance, and subtracted three thousand dollars. Whatever's left— that's my budget. The act of creating a reserve, even though I know I will violate it, makes it a budget. My house rehabbing had left me with $19,000 for furnishings. I subtracted $3,000 and linked my PayPal to my bank account, promising myself never to revert to my credit card.

Next I created averages for types of items. Averages allow me to play a bartering game with myself. It goes like this: Self to Self : "I'll give you the $125 art deco lamp if you promise to get the plain whale oil lamp, not the elegant one with cut glass." These bartering games so mimic parenting that they convince me I've got my inner child under control even though, of course, the act of playing the game is a clear indication that I haven't.

My budget required that I make a few adjustments to my mind map—to bring my associations into the land of my bank account. In my mind's eye, I might imagine my living room filled with antique scrimshawed dressing cases, yarn winders, pie crimpers, and walking sticks, but I can't afford them, even on eBay. The same applies to most genuine antique needlework samplers, most antique ship dioramas, and most antique woolies. These are wonderful, toy-like objects, that indeed grandchildren would enjoy . . . but, perhaps because they are too often associated with places like Nantucket, they are sought after by people with deeper pockets than mine.

So I try to steer my brainstorming away from Madison Avenue. In Nantucket terms, I want to be on the wrong side of the bluff—in Cod Fish Park. Those beautiful sailor's valentines—pink and purple shell gardens in handsome walnut hexagonal cases—have delightful Victorian dime store counterparts in the form of shell souvenirs. Those mahogany dressing cases, with ivory knobs and ebony and bone stars, have colorful hobo counterparts in the form of tramp art boxes. Eighteenth-century creamware, hand-painted and inscribed with the name of a whaling ship? Nope. Late Victorian Nantucket souvenir plates—Yep. Nineteenth-century maritime art—sailing vessels on turbulent seas? Too expensive. Nineteenth-century seascapes, crashing waves, rocks, gulls? Within reason. Fine nineteenth-century oil portraits of ship captains? No way. Fine nineteenth-century oil portraits of unknown men who look like ship captains but are actually from Lima, Ohio? You bet. Antique Nantucket lightship baskets? $1,000 or more. Antique Shaker-style baskets of similar style? $40–$50.

Limited funding isn't the only reason to look for inexpensive items on eBay. Another reason is, you relieve yourself from anxiety about whether something is a real antique gum box or not. For instance, scrimshaw is one of a group of items I would advise a person not to buy on eBay; there are too many fakes. Museum curators report that 90 percent of scrimshaw brought to them are fakes and it takes an expert eye and close, hands-on scrutiny to determine this. How could I distinguish a fake by viewing only photos?

Antique needlework is also frequently replicated, using a tea bath to "age" it. Often the key to determining if needlework is old is looking at the back if it is mounted and framed. Old needlework is folded over and nailed onto thin strips of wood. Wood usually reveals its age. So does the raw canvas. A good seller usually photographs the back of anything framed but if that's not the case, just ask. Many "antique" ship dioramas were made in the first half of the twentieth century or later so if you apply the British definition of antique: 100 years or older, they are technically "vintage."

"Watch out for all the fakes on eBay" is the warning of most retail antique dealers, trying to win back some of the territory they have lost to cyber-shopping. "This one is real," a dealer will tell you, "not like all the fakes you see on eBay." Should the fact that there are lots of fakes in circulation among "antiquers" keep you from buying on eBay? Well, all I can say is that the biggest, most expensive fake I've ever bought, I bought in a very tweedy London antique shop. It was not an eighteenth-century highboy, but a twentieth-century reproduction of one. I should have known better—the drawers weren't even dove-tailed. But here's the thing. The American antique restorer who documented my case for fraud, pointed out that I had paid what it was worth. I'd paid far too little for what it pretended to be.

## 1

Certainly, educate yourself about the objects you're looking for. Your education can begin on eBay itself. Don't get too excited about the first little antique thing-a-ma-bob you see. Copy and paste the key words you find in its listing and see if you can find similar ones listed (as I did the corn planter). If there are too many and if they are identical, well . . . at the very least, you've learned something about their rarity—an indicator of value. Now exit eBay and do some online research. Find trustworthy antique dealers, who list similar objects; find antique encyclopedias and chapters in antique books; Google your way to finding entries on, say "How to identify a fake corn planter." Nine times out of ten your Google search will not be in vain.

## 2

Never pay very much for the first antique example you buy on eBay.

You'll learn a lot from your first purchase, but you don't want the lesson to be painful. Here's a weird example of what I mean. One of my earliest purchases was an old mechanical toy. The description read "it really works!" When it arrived, I tried it and it didn't work. So I emailed the seller. He emailed back, "I never said it worked, the box did." He had simply transcribed the claim written on the side of the box. Should I have shot back, like the teacher that I am, "BUT YOU DIDN'T USE QUOTATION MARKS!" Hmmmm.

I had paid too much for a broken mechanical toy and my pride was hurt.

But I decided to swallow it as a lesson learned. In the future I would send a question before purchasing something that "works." My question would be, "Who says?"

## 3

Until you become very familiar with the type of object you are purchasing, bid what you would pay for the item, even if it were a fake. In other words, if you like how it looks, you might want to own it, even if it's not authentically old, or by a famous designer—as long as you didn't pay too much. Take "antique oriental rugs" for example.

Over time, I purchased about a dozen of them for my house. They are lovely. Usually they were described as dating from the 1930s or earlier. Additionally, they are allegedly from Iran, or Afghanistan, sometimes Turkey. Frankly, I don't care if they were made much more recently, or if they were made in India. I never paid more than $300 for them and they are beautiful. IKEA or Pottery Barn couldn't match them at twice the cost.

Why are eBay furnishings so affordable? Why did I decide not to buy my furnishings from island antique stores, auctions, or yard sales? Aside from the lovely fact of convenient indexing, which I have already mentioned, there are a few other reasons for using eBay. As politically incorrect as it sounds, the first option I omitted is buying locally, and that would hold for many resort towns besides Nantucket. It may be the case that one is always better off buying items of indigenous interest to a place, at the farthest point from that place—especially if the average median income of summer residents is the GNP of a small country. East Timor would probably be a terrific place to buy a Victorian Nantucket souvenir cup. Even your hometown would be a better place to buy a Nantucket item.

If you don't understand this principle, think about your impulse to buy souvenirs at a theme park like Disney World. You're two minutes from the greatest high of your life on Splash Mountain—where those robotic banjo-playing frogs, ducks, and especially that goofy bear made you forget your unpaid health insurance premium. You're still singing "Zip-a-Dee-Doo-Dah," as you amble into the souvenir shop with the most darling kids ever born. You decide to buy a red and white polka dot kerchief tied to a stick, like the one Brer Rabbit was carrying, which you then, for the rest of your vacation, use to carry snacks in and which you even carry onto the plane, but, once home, shove onto the top shelf of your closet. How much would you charge for that at a yard sale? Fifty cents?

Summer places are as good as theme parks. The happiness you experience is so great that, like love, it wants to give birth—to a product, to a possession that you like to think

a very plain 3.5-inch creamer (no gold trim) depicting the Martha's Vineyard–Nantucket steamship is $110. Poor Newark vase. All the gold leaf, like all the granite countertops and dentil crown molding, can't overcome the old adage, "location, location, location."

embodies your happiness. But of course it doesn't embody it really. Out of context, that possession is almost valueless. The Nantucket items I have bought on eBay were affordable because they were from Kansas, Florida, Maine, New York, and Clinton, Massachusetts. Even then, they weren't exactly cheap. In the last ten or fifteen years, the word has spread as far as Kansas that Nantucket spells money. An eBay seller in Maine, specializing in Victorian souvenirs from all over the Northeast, lists a very lovely "Buy it Now" German, 5-inch antique vase (with gold trim) commemorating Newark, New Jersey at $14.95; while

## 4

Because there is no longer a middleman to share in the profit. Adam Cohen writes at length about this in his fascinating book *The Perfect Store* (see pp. 106-110 in Cohen's book). eBay put antique dealers in competition with their pickers—people who supplied them with "finds" from flea markets, garage sales, country auctions. These pickers are now selling directly on eBay.

## 5

Because shopping at your local antique store creates a sense of scarcity (and thus higher value) but a global marketplace makes quantities visible and thus often less valuable. Here's an example of this principle. My first encounter with tramp art came in a little antique shop in Frenchtown, New Jersey. I'd been rummaging around antique stores for thirty years but never seen anything like it. The price for the medium sized box was $398.00. Very cool but too expensive for me. Remembering that box, "tramp art" was one of the first antique "categories" I tried out when I began searching eBay. Tramp art was everywhere! But no, it wasn't everywhere really. On closer look, the listings were mostly from Germany and the Netherlands, and from places those trampy German immigrants went, like Missouri, Wisconsin, Michigan, and East Stroudsburg, Pennsylvania. Now that so much of tramp art was accessible to what had been remote markets, it was less expensive. The box in New Jersey was the only one I'd ever seen, and it was so unusual, I might have bought it if it had been a good day for my

bank account. Now I've seen so many cool tramp art boxes on eBay, I'm demanding that they whistle and turn cartwheels.

# 6

Because the auction format can almost guarantee sales, which means a seller can decide to live on smaller profit margins, but greater sales quantities. In other words, eBay can function like Walmart for sellers with sufficient quantity—sellers, for example, who specialize in estate liquidations. How many times have you walked into an antique store that was so quiet, you found yourself whispering for fear of disturbing the owner who has made it through half of *War and Peace* since the last customer? You pick up a china thimble and ask the price, knowing that either it will be $385 so he can pay the rent, or it will be $10 and he'll be tempted to throw it at you if he's sat there all afternoon and that's all you're going to purchase.

# The Trustworthiness of eBay

I may have decided to furnish my house on eBay because of cost, but I soon learned that there was a much sweeter advantage to this route—I entered a community of very nice people. Indeed, I soon felt that I had found the relatives I had always wanted—a rowdy bunch of garrulous cousins with lots of cool stuff. If you've spent much time on eBay you know exactly what I mean by cousins. Rowdy we'll get to in a minute. Given a multiple choice survey in which you are asked to choose an analogy for "eBayer" relationships, which would you choose?

## A

Sales person/customer. Of course not. What sales person slips a little shell decorated pin into the packing box with a handwritten note that says, "Thought you would enjoy this too."

## B

Middle Eastern merchant/tourist? Close, they share the idea that a business transaction should also involve a friendly engagement. But eBay sellers don't comment on the weather, or flatter you by claiming the leather to be as soft as your cheek— they tell you what just happened to them at the supermarket this morning.

## C

Friend/friend? Not really. eBayers are as diverse as the American population. Much as you like them, you tend to have nothing objective in common with "Eurostuff" or "Bleeding gums" or "themerchantofdennis" or "cattledog."

## D

Cousin/cousin? Bingo. You may have nothing in common with your cousins from Albuquerque but they are more likely to pitch in and cut you some slack than the average contender for a seat on the bus. That's how 99.9% of eBayers are.

*After spending two months on eBay, furnishing my house, I talked like a political candidate returning from the campaign trail. "eBay sellers are the most honest, hard-working, friendliest bunch you could ever want to meet," I told all my friends, behind whose indulgent smiles I could see a hint of concern at my recent loss of cynicism. Buying on eBay was genuinely heartening. I really mean it.*

*7*

*The*

*Living*

*Room*

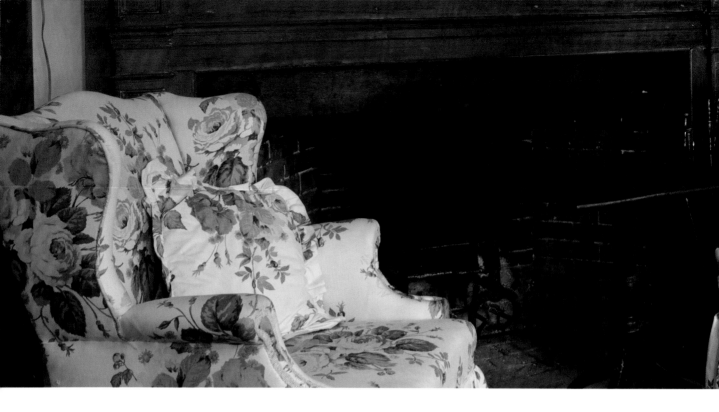

When I think back on our time spent in Rosemary's living room, the scene is always a variation on life in a turtle terrarium. You know the kind. One turtle is basking under a plastic palm tree (my brother); another is waddling in the water (my sister); another is upside down (uh oh) on a rock (me); another is moving on top of the closest turtle (my other brother).

To clarify: on any given day my brother might have just invested $1.50 in a bamboo backscratcher: a stick with a small curve at one end shaped vaguely like a hand. He would be stretched out on the sofa, his feet on one of its velvet arms, employing this new piece of technology to scratch his shoulder and spine in a dramatic

display of the good life. My younger sister might be on the floor with a Cinderella coloring book, her crayons scattered all over the Oriental rug next to her. I would be reading in a chair next to my favorite American Brilliant crystal lamp. My second brother, entering with a bowl of popcorn, would inevitably begin to engage in a tussle to gain a spot on the sofa. Some deal would be struck—if he can make ten kernels of popcorn land on Cinderella's nose, he can push my brother's feet off the couch. Multiple life forms coexisting in the same space—Rosemary's living room deserved the name.

Not so our living room back in the suburbs of Philadelphia. There, homework meant that my siblings and I were condemned to a form of solitary confinement in our respective

bedrooms. Our paths crossed in restless recess only at the dinner table or in the kitchen waiting for plates to be served. At the other side of the front hall, our living room was as inviting as the front parlor of a funeral home. Its silk brocade chairs had feather cushions that blew up like blowfish and like blowfish threatened anyone who dared to sit on them with the impossibility of ever restoring them to their primped beauty. Every few months dinner guests were given permission to enter the room and we might be invited in to make a round of introductions before slipping upstairs—no living within those walls. To make a living room that invites living, I operated from certain premises, derived, no doubt from that Rosetta Stone of my aesthetic wisdom —Rosemary.

1 Every chair deserves a table to put a drink on and a lamp to read by.

2 All seating must be comfortable so there is no musical chairs for a decent place to sit.

3 A couch is for stretching out on as well as sitting upright in.

4 A rug should be soft enough for lying and kneeling on and designed for camouflaging marks and spills. This pretty much means it should be an Oriental.

5 Every chair deserves something interesting to look at. And that doesn't mean looking at the person opposite you.

6 Games, books and sketch pads should be easily accessible.

The Heirloom House

The second premise is as important as the first: It should recall the living that came before us. The room should invite us to remember and, at times, escape into the past.

1. If you're lucky enough to have a fireplace in a room you should not put a television screen in it or above it. Ideally you should find another room to dedicate to film and television.

2. Paintings should allow for flights of fantasy.

3. Lamps should recall flickering flames, smoldering wicks.

4. Chairs should have worn runners from rocking or arms softened by the embroiderer's elbow, the pipe smoker's wrist.

5. Collections should reflect a bygone generation's happy hours of creative craft.

One of my first dinner guests, sitting in my newly furnished living room, remarked thusly about my living room décor: "So, your drapes are a print that doesn't match the print of your sofa which doesn't match the print of the Queen Anne chair ... would you say that you are postmodern?"

*Really?*

*Postmodern? Me?*

Who knew that chintz and toile could be Postmodern? To me they are classically 1940s and 1950s summer house in style. Since the outside of my house is covered in pink roses during the summer, it seemed an excellent idea to have them spill over onto the living room furniture. However, the risk of flowered chintz is that it will make a room look like a woman's boudoir, not so much excluding men as ignoring them. So I wanted the curtains to be a rather coarse blue and off-white toile—as masculine as a toile could get. I didn't want a plain color, because that would simply act as a backdrop to the floral chintz. A masculine blue and white print would balance out the pink flowered chintz. So maybe you could call that postmodern in my pursuit of gender equality.

# Wall Shelves

I learned the power of a single shelf from drooling over images of Carl Larsson's home in Sweden. He had them everywhere—on top of doors, along the headboards of beds, tucked in a corner on a stairwell. They were painted white or his favorites: milky green and blood orange. Some held books; some held cups and plates, some plants, some a row of framed prints or paintings. Shelves were also one of Underhill's favorite talking points. Everywhere-a-shelf linked 'Sconset village seaside huts with their ship forebears. The link wasn't mere nostalgia; shelves were a necessity where floor space was too limited for tables and bureaus. Where else are you going to put your plates, your beer mugs, your socks, if not on the wall?

I have to admit, my love of a shelf is more aesthetic than practical. The floor space in my Nantucket house can contain a few tables and bureaus; but the lines of a nice old table are lost when you pile objects on it, to say nothing of losing the expansive gleam of waxed and polished wood.

Moreover, shelves give walls texture; they contribute greater dimensionality than paintings. In that respect, they balance out the array of shapes (furniture) that decorate the floor. As we have seen, Underhill applied this principle of balance to his ceilings as well as his walls in the China Closet. No surface uncluttered . . . I meant unadorned . . . seems to have been his motto. I'm not that extreme; there has to be a clear path in case Gene Kelly drops in and wants to perform "Singing in the Rain" on your living room ceiling. Imagine the mess he would have made in Underhill's cottage.

Once you have your shelf, the arrangement of items on it becomes an exercise in composition and color and even theme— potentially all the elements of a work of art. You don't have to think of it as simply a place where objects in your collection go. And you don't have to keep collections segregated by shelf. You can think of a shelf as a Cornell box of sorts, a composition of "found art."

One of my shelves became a study in brown.

Since our ancestors seem to have valued shelves more than we do, eBay is a wonderland of them. You can search simply "antique hanging shelf" or you can add "carved wood" or you can be more specific about era and style by keying in "antique Eastlake"(for shelves with multicolored wood and saw-toothed edges) or "Mission" (for shelves with slats like old sleds), "Black forest" (for shelves with deer heads ) "Victorian" (for shelves with scaffolding, pillars and railings) or "tramp" (for shelves with gouged patterns). Most of my shelves were classified as "antique Eastlake."

The Heirloom House

# Curtains

More and more people consider buying furnishings for their homes on eBay—lamps, antique boxes, candlesticks etc . . .  but there are still many home-decorating categories that are barely discovered—vast wastelands where only one or two bids occur in a seven-day listing. These online frontiers include hand-painted ceramic tiles, vintage bedspreads, and custom draperies. Week after week, die-hard pioneers set up shop in these categories, often with remarkable wares, and week after week, very few e-travelers pass through. Two out of the three examples I mentioned (curtains and tiles) require installation. That may be the inhibitor. Well that's just silly. Buy on eBay and hire an installer if you're scared to do it yourself.

Perhaps my favorite pioneer in the frontier lands of eBay is Tyra, my curtain supplier. True to my metaphor, she lives in a small town in the Western state of Oregon. She

set up shop there, in what she calls a hardscrabble area for three reasons: First, the cost of living was low; second, outsourcing had left plenty of unemployed seamstresses for hire and third, the internet opened the door to non-local markets. I came across her fabric choices by searching "custom draperies toile." As often happens, after reviewing her beautiful toile choices I clicked her other "items for sale" and feasted my eyes on her entire collection of chintzes, barkcloths, damasks, botanical prints on linen, brocades, sculpted chenille, Waverly fabrics, jacquard and cotton sateen . . . She sells sets of 4 or 6 or 8 panels that are lined and rod-pocketed and made to your measurements in length, each panel being fifty inches in width. She made all the curtains for my house—five sets of beautifully classic fabrics that fit snuggly on my rods and kiss the floors gently and make every room fresher, softer, and certainly more beautiful.

In the process of making my third purchase from Tyra's site, I received an email from her recommending that I withdraw my offer on a pattern. "You won't like it. Trust me," she wrote so forthrightly that I immediately arranged with her to receive a refund. To substitute for the one I had purchased, she sent me photos of three fabrics in similar hues she was sure I would like much better. I selected from them. Later I was too curious not to ask why she had dissed the one I'd selected. "I know your taste. The pattern was too big." I loved the curtness of her reply. It bespeaks the confidence of the real professional that she is. Go to her site. See what I mean. stores.ebay.com/Applebox-Company

# Thumb latches/ antique hardware

Twist a doorknob and you know you're not in Nantucket's whaling era anymore. The first US patent for a doorknob was filed in 1878. Before then the thumb latch announced your entrance with an upward *click* and a downward *clang*. The handle might be iron or brass, softly curved, or firmly square but in any case allowing a full grip, a hearty handshake. *Click* then *clang* versus just *click*. No contest. Sound, touch, sight converge creating a motor memory recalling the sound that announced a Nantucket whaler's return home.

On eBay, search "antique thumb latch." At between $19 and $29 the price is the same as new reproduction hardware. And you get free rust!

# Shell Art

Before I became acquainted with the work of my eighteenth- and nineteenth-century shell obsessed counterparts, I used to prepare for summers at the shore by visiting my local cigar stores and buying empty boxes for a dollar each. I also bought simple wood frames and spray painted them white. Summer after summer at the beach, before

folding beach chairs and collapsing the umbrella, we'd shake off the drowsiness of a nap in the sun, grab a bucket and scavenge the surf's edge for shells. Within a few days of residency, our dining table could not be used for dining. It was a field of shells, waiting to be fit into patterns like pieces of a jigsaw puzzle.

Shells are great for patterning because while they vary in shape, size and color, within their species, they don't vary much at all. These little calcium houses made by sea creatures have all the conformity of the nineteenth-century Nantucketers' wood-shingled houses. My children and I would form little Levittowns of them in the usual fashion, lining them up in rows, ranch houses first (small scallop shells), then 1960s geodesic domes (snails), then a few Victorian gothic extravaganzas (conchs). Lucky for us that when we're asleep at night, some large hand doesn't reach down and pick up our wood box house, shake out the soft-skinned inhabitants and carefully glue it to a large meteoroid, a decorated bauble to celebrate the Apocalypse.

Apparently my love of shell crafts is trifling compared to your average Victorian's. The perfect illustration of this is the fact that one of the world's major oil companies developed out of a nineteenth-century shell trading business. Guess which one.

The story of Shell Oil serves as the perfect illustration of the nineteenth century's appetite for shells. A Jewish immigrant from Bavaria and Holland named Marcus Samuel set up a curio shop in East Smithfield, a slummy dock area on the outskirts of London. Included among his curios were shells and all manner of knickknacks adorned with them. Apparently the burgeoning development of resorts like Scarborough and Brighton in England caused shell-decorated souvenirs to be the nineteenth-century equivalent of salt water taffy.

To meet the wholesale demand of shopkeepers on piers and at expositions and fairs, Marcus employed forty women who did precisely what my children and I did at the kitchen table, only faster. Marcus also employed a handful of designers to come up with ideas for what these decorated things should be. Their conclusion?

Pretty much anything.

Shells covered almost every unnecessary object a Victorian was likely to feel the need for: needle cases, glove boxes, match holders, pin cushions, letter holders, dioramas, miniature dog houses, boxes for nothing in particular, ink bottle stands, miniature furniture, mirrors, frames. Without doubt this was the ultimate in kitsch for nineteenth-century holidaymakers.

By 1851, Marcus Samuel had made a small fortune on this kitsch and had moved his family to a handsome house on prosperous Finsbury Square in London. His exports were diversifying—he also exported cotton and machinery—and his web of trade extended all over the Far East. Marcus Samuel himself didn't engage in the oil trade, but after he died, his son

Marcus Jr. did, importing lamp oil for starters. While the company now had major clients in Canada, the US, and Japan, buying silks, grains, lamp oil, and cotton, it never abandoned its little shell boxes, which rewarded the company's loyalty by becoming so popular that a new shell decorating factory was built in Wapping and a Paris branch of the trading company was licensed to sell "shell-work, trinkets and ornaments in shell-work," the distinction between which is not at all clear to me. And finally, as the ultimate tribute to its founding fathers, when the Shell Oil Company launched its first oil tankers, they were named "Conch," "Clam" and "Cowrie."

None of which answers the question of why it is that I bought upwards of thirty antique, very kitsch shell souvenirs on eBay, when ceramic bunnies pushing wheelbarrow planters stopped quickening my pulse when I was seven. Is it the patina old objects attain, that golden glow of old shellac on shells, or is that simply a tautology: I love old kitsch because it looks old. Or is it because old souvenirs are deeply poignant. All these cherished "keepsakes" no longer prompt the particular memory that gave them life. But in losing that specificity, they become deeply abstract, testimonials to the human desire to hold on to what's fleeting—to holidays, summers, young love, memory itself.

My favorite purchase in the realm of Victorian shell art could not have come from Marcus Samuel's factory, or anybody's factory, because it is messy, clunky, full of incongruities and more or less bears the signature of its eleven-year-old creators in the form of faded photographs under cracked glass. I paid all of $28 for it and when it arrived, it looked like it had been stored in a mechanic's garage where every other day a rag covered in grease landed on it. I scrubbed its shells and beads and odd little figurines with a soft toothbrush. It still looks fairly ragged, a child's effort no doubt eliciting the kind of euphemistic praise mothers resort to in order not to lie: "It looks like you worked really hard on that." The girls beam back.

A more sophisticated amateur made the other piece of shell art I treasure. It is very much like a sampler in shells and seaweed. A fairly awkward poem is handwritten in two types of ink, the gold ink having faded to shadow:

*Call us not weeds, we are flowers of the sea,*

*for lovely and gay tinted are we*

*And quite independent of sunshine and*

*showers. Then call us not weeds, we are*

*ocean's gay flowers.*

Often eighteenth-century ladies created shadow-boxed flower arrangements out of shells. But this arrangement of shells and seaweed forms a ship's anchor. Was it made by a sailor for his sweetheart back home? Was he trying to prepare her for his watery grave by promoting the sea's beauty? Was it she who was creating a keepsake for her sailor, cheering him along with a consoling poem? The imagined memories I attach to this piece of shell art are layered beneath a real memory that is much more banal.

Because of the picture's delicacy, I asked the eBay seller to hold it until I could pick it up in person. The vendor lived off of Route 95, just north of New Bedford. We met in the parking lot of a mall, using cell phones to navigate our way to an area with two empty parking spaces. I had no time to spare as I was trying for a 1:55 ferry. I pulled my car in next to hers; we both popped our trunks, got out, passed the framed picture from one nest of starter cables to another, slammed shut the trunks and went our separate ways. I couldn't shake the sense of having engaged in a drug exchange. Every once in a while I pass the picture hanging in my dining room and imagine the seaweed morphing into *weed* weed.

# Dioramas

Though geographically irrelevant to my Nantucket house, a collection of souvenir dioramas from New Mexico and Arizona adorns the wall of one of its bathrooms. Another bathroom amuses occupants with a collection of Great Lakes souvenirs—tree-trunk slices hand-painted with landscapes. The scale of these small works of art perfectly suits a bathroom. Think about it. In most bathrooms . . . well, in my bathrooms . . . .you're never more than two or three feet away from a wall, and you're alone (usually), and occupied with something mindless (teeth brushing, peeing, blow-drying). The conditions are perfect for settling your gaze on a miniature desert scene, complete with highway, and, in some cases, Jesus, and taking yourself back to whenever you had the slightest acquaintance with that soulfully lonely kind of journey. The miniaturization of worlds, whether it be in snow globes, terrariums, train sets, ships in bottles, framed shadow-boxes, always invites us

in for some reason. We wait patiently outside, like Alice in Wonderland, as though some magic key or potion will adjust our scale to suit the walk we want to take along that path.

# Bark Bottles

If you are interested in collecting shell art or tramp art or scrimshaw or maritime paintings or toleware or decoys or taxidermy or decoupage or antique embroidery or even needle cases or snuff boxes—inevitably you can find a couple of books to serve as guides. But if you are interested in collecting Bark Bottles, forget it. You won't even find an online site devoted to it. Sure, there are plenty of books on bottle collecting, but Bark Bottles don't merit even a chapter.

So what are Bark Bottles? Well, that's the problem. I don't know.

Everyone who has ever handled my bark bottle collection has a different theory about how they're made. Concerning why they are made, there is absolute agreement—they're very cool. Why is making a bottle look like a tree branch very cool? Because we like things that conceal, disguise, even trump their function (with all due respect to Howard Rourke). We like Murphy beds, convertible sofas, Bible flasks, mouse tail measuring tapes, chicken purses, cupcake dolls, fish mouth bottle openers, spaceship telephones, dog boot scrapers, strawberry pin cushions. The more incongruous the better. So while antique bottles shaped like high top boots are fairly enticing (and popular among collectors), the radical dichotomy between rough tree bark and smooth glass is truly delicious.

I like them even more because one has the sense that they are someone's personal bottle, customized, easily identified—like a monogrammed flask but oh so much dearer because self-made. Which brings us back to the question of how they are made:

### Construction theory #1:
They are made by covering bottles with clay and then shaping the clay to look like a tree branch and painting it. Not possible. Some of my bark bottles have woodworm.

### Construction theory #2:
They are made from a mixture of glue and sawdust, not clay, which explains the woodworm. Otherwise the shaping and painting are the same as above.

### Construction theory #3:
They are made by taking a real branch, slightly larger than the bottle you want to surround, hollowing the branch, soaking the branch in water, and then slipping it like a sleeve over your bottle and letting it shrink to form. The proponent of this theory was Joyce Wadler, the *New York Times* journalist who wrote an article about my Nantucket house. She is a professional writer with a lot of imagination.

### Construction theory #4:
They are made from chewing tobacco, well masticated and then applied by hand all around the bottle. Let dry. I would have raised an eyebrow at this explanation had I not tried to wrestle clumps of spat-out chewing tobacco from an old crocheted quilt my grandfather sent me. Rock hard and adhering like barnacles to pilings, the stuff is so strong you could build a house out of it if you could just gather enough chewers.

# Tramp Art

The first bark bottle I came across
was listed under "Tramp Art" on
eBay. It was not what is conventionally
called tramp art, but as you can
see from my collection, I don't
regret the sloppiness of the lister.
The term *tramp art* is somewhat
elastic on eBay anyway. Under that
search heading you will find lots of
crafty things made out of humble
materials like popsicle sticks,
matches, shells, bottle caps,
walnut shells, gum wrappers,
cigar bands, cloves, pebbles . . .
but the real tramp art connoisseur
is searching for objects made out
of beautifully gouged cigar boxes.
It's a strangely evolved form of
whittling and for that reason
belonged in my summer associations
with layman's crafts. I have never
tried whittling, but, like any lover
of Westerns, I've bought into the
mystique of it. It's what a man's hands
do when his mind is ruminating,

Sherry Lefevre

or as Cheyenne puts it in *Once Upon a Time in the West*:

> "He's whittlin' on a piece of wood.
> I've got a feeling when he stops
> whittlin' . . .
> Somethin's gonna happen."

The particular style of wood-carving called tramp art seems to have developed in Europe in the1860s and was popular through the beginning of the twentieth century, coinciding with the rising popularity of cigar smoking and their improved packaging—all those lovely wooden boxes with nothing to do. The simplest examples of tramp art consist of a single cigar box decorated with layers of notched wood strips in pyramid formations. The most complex examples involve multiple boxes and many, many little mountains of notched wood, as well as carved hearts, diamonds, pinwheels, birds, crosses, ivory inlays, hardware, velvet, mirrors etc. etc.

As to the origin of the tramp art name, there are two schools of thought. Some insist that it was so

named because it was itinerants or "tramps" who took to it, creating gift-wares they could sell along their train-hopping way. But the counter theory argues that there were plenty of notchers who stayed put—working out of wood shops in small towns and cities. To sell their wooden wares they'd have to do some "trampin" around, ergo the name. Evidence supporting the vagabond theory of tramp artists is just beneath the surface of today's eBay listings. They seem to follow the Oregon Trail. eBayers I purchased tramp art from lived in Missouri, Wyoming, and Washington State. Before eBay introduced me to antique dealers beyond the confines of my greater northeast, urban life, I had

only ever seen a single example of it. If those tramp artists were setting up woodshops, they weren't doing it in Philadelphia.

# Nautical Art

You can't have a seaside house without any paintings of the sea. It's a rule equivalent to creating an establishing shot in a film. Philadelphia's urban murals notoriously invite escapism into anywhere but the city which they adorn—autumnal woods, lakesides, even leagues under the sea; apparently W. C. Fields's sentiments about the city still prevail. But a vacation house's inhabitants don't want to be anywhere but where they are. Isn't that the point? They're happy to be reminded that they can walk out the door tomorrow and see waves crashing, foam spraying, gulls careening, sun and moon making sparkling paths of gold and silver to the horizon line. Many Nantucket houses have nineteenth-century ship portraits. The ships have the same trophy quality that permeates an equestrian's horse portrait. Wild as the beast or seas may be, the painting seems to assure, the right master (or owner) will conquer it. In spite of just sounding very snide,

I love them. But I can't afford them. Even on eBay.

What I can afford, it turns out, are seas without ships—beautifully executed paintings with dramatically roiling surf and rococo storm clouds, sublimely craggy cliffs and even, if you're lucky, a barely visible ship on the horizon. Nature, it seems, is less desirable than man on nature. We could get deeper into the psychology of that or we could just rejoice that another buyer's fear of impotence is our good luck.

My favorite seascape was painted by a Scot at the end of the nineteenth century. Its seller wrote a description that was wonderfully free of art-speak. There was no mention of texture, light, line, architectonic shapes and blah blah blah. Just, here's what I see and it's very cool:

*You'll be impressed by the pounding surf and the towering cliffs— even from a few feet away. But you won't really appreciate the quality of the work until you come in close for a look at the birds. I can't remember discovering another surf painting with such painstakingly executed birds—and SO MANY birds.*

*With that many birds, it must surely be a nesting area. Either that or something scrumptious is washing up onto the rocks and in the shallow waters.*

*This man most certainly knew his gulls. My guess? I'll bet he lived on the coast. I'd love to know something about him. Anyone know? Care to share?*

Sherry Lefevre

As it turned out, after I received the painting I was able to interpret the artist's name accurately (unlike the seller) and thereby learn something about him. Alex Mortimer (1885–1913) was a Scottish seascape painter known for his craggy cliffs and seagulls. And yup, he lived on the coast of Scotland. My seller was essentially right in seeing him for the gull aficionado that he was. And I will forever hear my own version of the seller's voice when I look at the painting: "What are those birds swarming after? Something scrumptious just washed up." LIKE WHAT! Aggghhhh!

My Mortimer seascape cost me $500—a real investment. I put a $200 cap on other art purchases. I bought five paintings from a dealer in Copenhagen who routinely listed beautiful period oil paintings— portraits, landscapes, seascapes, usually in their original gilt frames. His starting bid was $200 with a fairly standard shipping rate of $50. With about fifty listings a week, he often had no bidders. My purchases always resulted from having no competition as $200 was my limit. The paintings would arrive by FedEx three days after payment. I was so stunned with the beauty of my first purchase—a large 1930s oil of Copenhagen harbor, that I felt queasy. Was I buying stolen goods? Was my seller a fence for nimble thieves buying drugs in nearby Amsterdam? Probably not. There's a lot of old art in the world and only a little of it is sought after. The rest of it sells like used cars, for a fraction of what you would pay in a New York gallery for a current artist; deceased "listed" artists are a dime a dozen on eBay. What does that mean to contemporary artists? Stay alive!

# Ancestral Portraits

Every ancestral heirloom home needs a portrait ... or ten. Our paradigm for this is, of course, the ancestral houses of England, still in the "family" though sometimes loaned out for tours by mandate of the family accountant. Woburn Abbey is my personal favorite. Why? Because three thousand deer of various rare breeds surround it—a "collection" as it were. Since breeds of deer do not comingle, they are perfect for collecting as they maintain clear, albeit moving, distinctions to illustrate your range. My other reason for favoring Woburn Abbey is that the charming Dukes and Duchesses of Bedford managed to get themselves painted by Gainsborough and Reynolds.

To be authentic to the English paradigm, your portraits must depict your ancestors who once lived in your house and now linger on the walls, very much like haunting ghosts—the

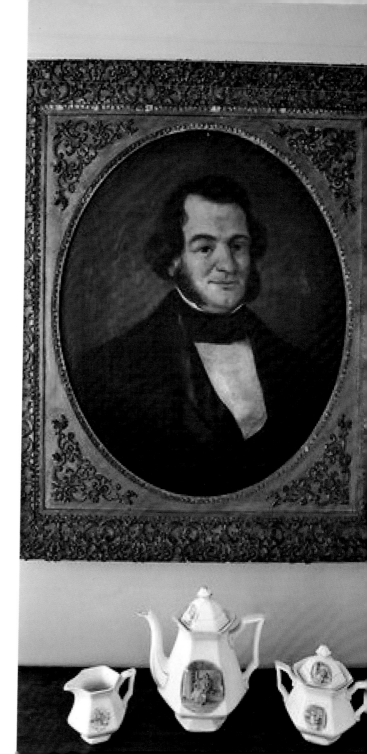

reason they are so easy to parody in haunted house horror films. Given that association, it may be a stroke of luck that most of us are not privileged to possess the real deal and thus must buy ancestors on eBay. Depending on the vitality of your imagination, your adopted ancestors may be less prone to haunt you, your blood carrying no trace of their poisoned dreams, their unrequited loves, their unpurged sins. Since in my case the once inextricable link between family, house and portraits has been severed in every way possible, I chose to piece things back together by finding portraits better suited to my house than to me. In other words, I tried to match them with the house's ancestry, not mine.

Nantucket houses are full of beautiful nineteenth-century portraits of ship captains, not the least bit finicky about being relocated from Salem, Massachusetts, or about being surrounded by a family from Atlanta, Georgia, so long as they are keeping dignified watch over a house with a widow's walk. But portraits of identifiable ship captains are pricey. It's much easier to find an affordable portrait of a man who looks like a ship captain but who is actually from Troy, New York, and whose ruddy cheeks and muttonchops are testimonials to cold mountain breezes rather than brisk salt air. Who's to know that my $200 purchase is not my house's second owner, Samuel Robbins, First Mate of the whale ship *Fabius*? In any case, my sitter has such an agreeable face, no one would have the heart to accuse him of being an impostor.

Pretty much any portrait done in the classic Great Masters style of portrait painting—rich, golden flesh surrounded by deep browns, like a crème caramel sitting in a chocolate mousse—is delicious as far as I'm concerned and there are many on eBay. Just a word of warning if you want to assure yourself of authenticity. The Chinese are great at imitating this style. Many Chinese vendors play it straight and offer you a picture of the original that they will copy. But inevitably these make their way from owner to owner and the provenance becomes vague. This is why dealers in authentic oil paintings photograph the backs—the stretchers, the aged pieces of wood, the weakened canvas backs, but even these features can be imitated. So back to my old adage—don't pay too much if you can't send it back.

## Ancestral photographs/tintypes

One of the thriftiest ways of owning a collection of nineteenth-century portraits is by purchasing antique painted tintypes on eBay. Tintypes were themselves the middle class's way of having a portrait "painted" in the mid-nineteenth century. An early form of photography, the image is developed on a thin iron (not tin) plate. Many customers were satisfied with the unadorned image but others wanted something that looked more like an artist's portrait, so the photographer, or an artist assistant, obliged by painting on top of the image. This was also, of course, the only way of giving the photograph color. The combination of amateur painting skills and photo-realism is, well, charming. Two rounded pads of china-pink cheeks, a collar of carefully traced white lace, waves of outlined-in-Sienna hair, surround piercing "real" eyes. The eyes of tintypes, peering out from their mask of paint, beg to speak. I managed to create a family out of an unrelated collection of painted tintypes. By grouping them around the game table on the upstairs landing, I gave gaming pastimes the air of a family tradition. Certainly the mid-nineteenth century was a good time for the game of checkers (the game made it to tournament status in 1848). So is 2014.

## Victorian needlepoints

A category of antique I can't afford (but wish I could) is the embroidered sampler. Odds are that one or two of the girls who grew up in my house in the 1800s stitched a sampler or two. They might even have included a picture of the house, a little square box with a tree next to it, under their rendering of the alphabet or a verse from the Bible. But rather than press my nose against my LCD screen to drool over what I can't afford, I've developed a gluttonous appreciation for all the sadly devalued needlework I *can* afford. Because, for

some reason, only samplers made by the eight-year-old Marys of the nineteenth century are worth anything. Everything Mary Wilson or Richards or Fuller or Hopkins made when she grew up is on eBay for a song.

The sentimentalism that makes samplers so charming is there in other forms of needlework—it was a "trending" emotion. Children and dogs . . . better yet children

*with* dogs were favorite subjects of needlepoint. If you couldn't hire Sir Edwin Landseer to paint your Spaniel like Queen Victoria did, you could buy a pattern of a Spaniel, Pug, St. Bernard, Poodle or Japanese Chin and needlepoint your own dog portrait. While not exactly original in every sense, your needlework expressed perfectly your care. Often these dogs sit on regal cushions or stand in the foreground of a vast estate as pompous in their portraits as their masters. I am stumped about whether the needle worker was as amused as I am to be mimicked by a dog.

Victorian needlework included other subjects: landscapes, portraits, lots of flowers or still lifes, reproductions of famous paintings. In many ways it was the paint by

medium falls a little short of the artist's, well, then see them as the ultimate in camp.

Search words for needlework on eBay include "wool work" and "Berlin work" as these are the terms Europeans use. Otherwise we Americans use "antique needlepoint" or "needlework" and "Victorian" can substitute for antique as well.

numbers of the nineteenth-century.

Needlework gave the rising industrial middle class art for their walls and (a measure of) artistic expression for their women. All of those nimble fingered people were like me . . . they wanted to have something they couldn't afford.  If their

# Games

I'm not a game player—I'm too restless—but sometimes I wish I were. It would be fun to shed this constant urge to do a project. So I wanted a game table to trigger thoughts of idling away time, as though one were driving through Idaho with mile after mile of unshaped hours ahead of you. I bought an old backgammon set to remember Arabs in a hookah bar, a vintage inlaid wooden chess and checkerboard to remember Parisians in Luxemburg Garden, and I bought sgreasy, yellowed playing cards to remember my grandmother at our kitchen table playing Solitaire. My house's first renters were a family with two young boys

who stayed for three weeks, during which time there were several terrific Nor'easters. The walls surrounding the game table were heavily marked from chair backs scraping and tipping and no doubt bucking back and forth in the turbulence of a tie-breaking win. Huzzah!!!! I shouted to myself. It worked!

As usual, my search for classic wooden game boards gave me glimpses of other vistas in vintage games, like a "worth a detour" route in a Michelin guide. The graphics on 1920s and 1930s board games are charmingly mundane examples of a great design era. For this reason I bought and framed the board from a game called Little Shoppers whose dice roll causes the player to land on a product, beautifully illustrated with full vintage label. Commercial products of this era are hotly collected precisely for these labels and here I have a game-land full of them. I hung the framed game board in the single bedroom as I anticipate mostly children sleeping there. A few other vintage games sit patiently in a blanket chest, casually tucked under Life and Monopoly, awaiting discovery. Their antique novelty, like old uniforms found in the attic, give them a lost treasure quality, or so I like to think.

# 8
# Bedrooms

In vacation houses, bedrooms are for sleeping or reading in bed (or … whatever else you do in bed) but generally that's it. No one's going to hang out in a bedroom when they could be eating and drinking and enjoying the company of friends and family in the rest of the house. There's no need for a desk, thank God. There's no need for a dressing table either, given how tan and healthy you look. No need for a lounge chair if you're lounging downstairs. So vacation house bedrooms can be quite small and cozy.

In the spirit of the old whale houses and Underhill cottages, I made my bedrooms smaller than they were at purchase. In one case minimizing a bedroom allowed the upstairs landing to have a window and thus a sweetly

lit communal area where I put my game table and four chairs. The staircase and landing are much airier and more welcoming as a result. And frankly, the bedroom is much cozier and welcoming as well. It contains twin beds that tuck under eaves with exposed split wood panels and rafters. Within a Quaker-style Nantucket house, it feels like you have entered a log cabin. The original scale of the room took away this effect.

Another bedroom had an odd L shape and a single small window at the toe of the L, far away from the bed. It was wide enough for only a single bed under eaves. Ugh. It was clearly a bedroom designed by Dickens for an

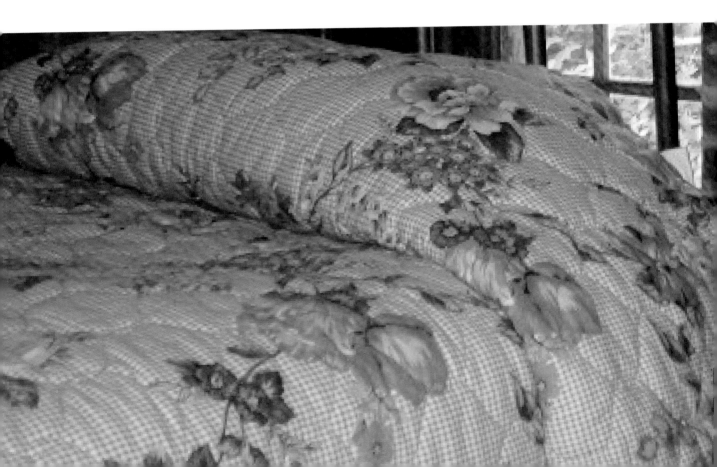

unfavored child. I decided to make it smaller still, cutting off its toe to create a master bathroom. And then I gave it a new window by the bed—a large one with beautiful curtains, so the smaller room seems bigger and certainly more loved.

Given the reduced functions of a bedroom, it's all the more important that it perform them well. Family and guests should see their rooms as the perfect place in which to read in bed and get a good night's sleep. That means great bedding; solidly framed beds (headboards to lean on); intimate reading lights; paintings next to the bed that take you places you'd want to go; bedside tables for books, water,

reading glasses, cordials and small Mission Arts and Crafts bookshelves for easy access to new or better perusing.

In the years before eBay, I had admired antique hook rugs in antique stores, but they were beyond my reach. Certainly no one in my income bracket bought Oriental rugs. And I had spent two years paying by installments for cotton chintz bedroom curtains that had cost almost $2,000. Now, on eBay, all these objects were affordable. My bedrooms could have antique hooked or Oriental rugs and chintz curtains.

## Bedspreads

If you rented a house at the beach in the 1960s, chances are the beds were draped in cotton chenille "popcorn" bedspreads. If not bleach white, these were light sherbert colors: white and pink or light blue and white, or, once in a while, pale green and white. They were lightweight and washable and their chenille patterns made them lie flat—no wrinkling, no ironing. Perfect for summer. I bought two of these on eBay for two of my beds. They might be forty years old but they look like they're new. They've already survived three summers of renters in Nantucket and they still look like new. At the same time I bought two white vintage/antique "matelasse" spreads (that happened to be "Bates" brand) for non-renter use. They have the same virtues as the chenille—bleachability and no-ironing necessary because of their trapunto surface. Trapunto is a technique used in embroidering or embellishing linens. A pattern is stuffed so that it rises off the surface. It's very elegant, especially when it's a

white on white design. The background is flat and only the pattern swells.

For my log cabin bedroom I wanted darker heavier bedspreads. I found a pair of vintage quilted, floral printed spreads that worked well with the curtains, but of course, weren't the same print—given my postmodern style.

Monogrammed Linens

For the sweet single bed—an old black iron one with brass knobs—I found a simple 1930s cotton top-sheet, with a beautiful embroidered monogram. Monograms are one of my favorite searches in eBay's indexing. You can enter "antique vintage linen monogram (your initial)" as a search and find whatever wonderful guest towels, pillow sham, napkins, bedspreads . . . just happen to contain your initials. Although the other letter in this coverlet's monogram is not in my family, the principal last initial "L"

is mine. So I have imagined the J to stand for Jennifer—a name I like not simply because I like Jenny Lind beds. Jennifer Lefevre rhymes, but not obnoxiously, and suggests a girl with just the right amount of sass.

## Wastebaskets

When people furnish rooms, they often create needless hierarchies. They give high priority items more time and a bigger allowance. This leads to a form of social stratification within a single room—a class society in which sofas lord it over side tables and everything lords it over the humble wastebasket. Frankly, there's no room in a room for such rampant discrimination. Not only is that wastebasket as visible as anything else, but it performs an invaluable service and often engages friends, family,

guests, more intimately than other items in the room. This is why, in my list of furnishings to purchase on eBay, I didn't overlook "vintage wastebaskets." In fact they were some of my happiest purchases. In years past, people knew the value of a well-decorated metal cylinder. Some were hand-painted with flowers and are listed as tole; others were embellished with a very rudimentary form of decoupage—a single paper print, or litho, coated in varnish. The first of these that ever caught my attention was a wedding gift I received—it was a custom order from a local Philadelphia gift shop. My wedding invitation had been carefully glued to a metal wastebasket and outlined in gold leaf. Hmm. Apparently this was considered classy on The Main Line. I have to say, the connotations didn't work for me.

# Lamps

An unadulterated nineteenth-century house has no overhead lighting, of course. Candles and whale oil lamps would have provided whatever the sun didn't afford in my house. Now it takes about four electric lamps per room. In the living room I needed six. That made for a lot of eBay lamp hunting. My searches went in three directions—Whale oil lamps that I could electrify and nautical lamps that were either

gimbal or featured ship wheels.
I viewed a lot of ship lanterns on eBay but ultimately resolved that they should not make the transition from wall to table.

Whale oil lamps are in healthy supply on eBay. The Buy-it-Now prices are high—in the $175 to $350 range. But most of the auctions end at about $45.00. Electrifying a whale oil lamp is easy. Most hardware stores sell kits with sockets, cords and harps that will sit on top of the lamp where the wick holder used to be. If you're a purist, keep the brass wick holder for posterity. In any case, the purist should be somewhat assuaged that the electrification does not (should not) involve boring a hole in the glass or brass or whatever comprises the body of the lamp.

Lamps with nautical iconography: ship's wheels, lighthouses, whales, salty-dog fishermen in foul-weather gear, are all over eBay but the trick is to navigate around molded plastic kitsch. There's a lot of nautical kitsch—lamps you might find in a seafood restaurant next to the mint bowl. Not that there's anything wrong

with that, just not in my house. So, as usual, the older the ship wheel lamp was, the more I liked it. Maybe kitsch is really just a form of varnish that wears off with time.

Gimbal lamps are hinged in such a way that the light will stay upright even as the boat pitches and heaves in rough seas. Real gimbal lamps sit on two connected pivoting spheres that allow the lamp to respond to the ocean's movement—in any direction. The more common gimbal lamp can only pivot forward or back. It is made to hang on a wall or sit on a table and still keep its poise . . . as long as those seas don't require a pirouette. I love them. While my house is relatively stable, it often feels like it is rocking. When storms hit the island, they do so with such intensity, you could imagine needing to tie yourself to a tree or a nearby fireplug. Add to that the fact that our houses are made of sticks, more or less, sitting on ground that is 50 percent sand, and it's easy to feel that, in the grand, geological scheme of things, we're a fragile, transitory little spec in a great ocean. So it is that, when the howling winds rattle my windows and doors and roof and walls, it's a comfort to sit up in bed, with a good book, knowing that my gimbal reading lamp, nailed on the wall next to me, will stay upright.

# Bookshelves

Bookshelves need to be treated separately from hanging wall shelves, because they are not so much an aesthetic consideration as an infinitely functional one. On eBay (of course) I bought a small bookshelf for every bedroom. True, there is also a set of book-laden shelves in the "gathering room" or den, but that in no way obviates the need for additional shelves in the bedrooms. Why? Because (according to me) it's one of the nicest things you can give the friends and family who are visiting you. It beats mints on the pillow and flowers on the bedside table. Better than a browsing table at a bookstore, it can offer up very personal and specific paths to happiness. It can offer solace to the insomniac and company to the afternoon napper. But don't people bring their own reading material, you ask? Yes of course they do. But that appears to be irrelevant.

I conducted a study to support this claim. Over the past year, a myriad of guests have stayed in the Nantucket house. Without any hint or encouragement on my part, not a single one has failed to pick up a book from his or her bedroom bookshelf. I have observed a bookshelf book being carried staggeringly to the coffeemaker in the morning, or to the living room couch where it is laid on the coffee table while the borrower stretches out and adjusts a blanket around his/her legs. I have seen these books wander out to the back garden chaise and found them on bathroom shelves next to toilet paper.

This is in spite of everyone's having brought their own paperback, or their own Kindle with the whole library of Congress at their disposal. So why do they nestle up with my books? The reason is probably too deep in the human psyche to fathom in any but a superficial way. It lies somewhere between why we like to reach over with our fork and sample someone else's dish, even before we have tasted the one we ordered, and why we can't fix our own insomnia but can make a hundred recommendations to our friends. Whatever we have chosen for ourselves is tainted by familiarity. Maybe Groucho Marx got it right: we don't want to belong to a club that would take us.

Also, I own some very cool books.

I am rarely this narrow-minded, but when it comes to buying antique standing bookshelves, there is nothing that compares with an old Mission one. They are handsome and forthright, proving their sturdiness by showing off their pegged mortise and tenon joinery. They were made small enough for easy shipping and easy slipping into any sized room.

# Mirrors

As much as I like Venetian glass frames, or even rococo gilded frames, if they surround a mirror, the object screams vanity. My house's spirit is too Quaker for that. As in so many things, the nineteenth-century American and European craftsmen knew just how to make mirrors *look* modest (without really being so). They added a little landscape vignette to them. By all appearances your pause before the glass is not to admire yourself but to admire a little artistic achievement perched above your reflection.

Usually these mirrors are vertical rectangles made of turned wood, and the painting sits in its own frame at the top. The paintings are of the picturesque variety—rivers and mills, ruins and hills, boats and lakes or ships and waves. It's "reverse painted" on glass meaning that the paintings were created directly on glass to be seen through the unpainted side.

Forms were generally outlined in dark paint and color was a second layer. The procedure tends to make the paintings primitive—fine with me, especially for a multi-tasking object.

These are the kinds of mirrors I bought on eBay for my bedrooms and hallway. They are remarkably inexpensive for being so lovely. My search words were "antique Sheraton mirror" and "antique reverse painted mirror" and "antique Hitchcock mirror". You can alternate the words "Federal" and "nineteenth century" as well.

# Hooked Rugs

Antique hooked rugs are so beautiful and they're perfect for bedrooms. Their small size means you can surround a bed with them but they will not go under the bed where dust and moths like to gather. And their fragile nature prefers bedroom feet to any other. For beach houses, their rag loops don't operate the way pile does, swallowing sand like a Venus flytrap.

On top of all that, they are one of the antique categories that has undergone price devaluation on the Internet; eBay has become the place where all the antique hooked rugs from Maine to Pennsylvania to Wisconsin like to gather and thus form a riotously colorful mob that destroys their former elitism. I love their many styles from strangely modernist geometries to Arts and Craftsman scrolls to Deco florals.

## Oriental Rugs

For both bedrooms and sitting rooms I also wanted to buy old Oriental rugs, not so much because they are handsome, though of course they are, but because they are durable and they have an uncanny ability to camouflage dirt and stains. Renters, children, even friends with dogs should be welcome without furtive attention to their feet and food. I will never understand the popular choice of white or beige for beach houses.

"You bought your rugs on eBay?" friends have so often gasped that it's clear I've crossed the line of what a sane person should do. But my

became acquainted with a couple of eBay vendors who sold lovely and convincingly Persian rugs, I remained loyal to them and they to me . . . and over time, to my skeptical friends.

# Wool Throws

About the most hospitable thing you can do in a room is furnish it with a stack of really soft wool throws for easy access when the evening turns cool. You could graph the spike in sheer contentment that occurs when you dump a beautiful plaid blanket in someone's lap. Their pleasure at curling up in a chair and beginning to watch a DVD was at say, six, and now suddenly it becomes ten. Real wool blankets are crazy expensive to buy new, but on eBay they are a bargain. This may be because many buyers are reluctant to buy bedding that has touched strangers—a subliminal holdover from the days of smallpox infested blankets? Fear

approach was perfectly sane. I paid very little for my first purchases—a sum I would have been happy to part with regardless of whether the rugs were really from Iran or just from Pakistan or India. Once I of the more current contagion, bed bugs? Whatever phobia limits the competition for beautiful, dry-cleaned, pink and cream hand-woven blankets is ok by me. There are a few brand names associated with fine wool blankets that you can enter if you choose—Pendleton, Hudson Bay, Faribo—but old JC Penney wool blankets are wonderful too, and I purchased three hand-woven blankets for $9.99 each, without any label at all. The seller was a Canadian liquidating her in-laws' furnishings on eBay. She had found the blankets in a chest, apparently unused. I was the only bidder. In addition to fearing bedding infestations, Americans seem to fear foreign postal services. You will find that foreign listings on eBay are consistently valued at less than their American counterparts—even taking into account the increased cost of postage. Not suffering from this

weird little xenophobia, I've enjoyed the safe arrival of all the many foreign parcels I've purchased—without exception.

# 9
# Kitchens & Dining Rooms

I was delighted that my house's shed kitchen had a wood (not linoleum) floor and painted wood (not formica) cabinets. So I was surprised when my realtor told me that for summer rental, the house would need a new kitchen. The fact that all the appliances were in good working order had no bearing on the need to replace them. Apparently one of the characteristics distinguishing Nantucket renters from Margate, New Jersey renters is their appetite for SubZero meat.

In the last fifty years, no room in the house has become so elevated in status as the kitchen and no room has become so lacking in individuality. The mandate that countertops should be clear of clutter, as though we are all maintaining industrial work sites in our houses and it is our duty to leave the kitchen in as-found condition for the next shift, has removed the last traces of personal style. Gone are the seasoning racks; the tea, coffee, sugar, and flour canisters; the hanging pots; the drying herbs; the jars of pickled beets, the fruit bowls and potato baskets; the message slates; the copper pots filled with spatulas and wooden spoons. The everyday evidence of food and life is hidden inside cabinets or better yet, part of the interior architecture of pullout shelves and drawers. Even kitchen appliances have disappeared into paneled cabinetry that has gone from stained to pickled to painted with a conformity known only in the world of hemlines. Countertops go through the same rapid, post-Formica, must-have

trend cycles, and brands of faucets have become a wealth-indicator as fetishistic as watches. Who'd have thought that as a generation, we'd be admiring each other's showerheads?

Click on any listing of Nantucket houses for sale and you will see the same kitchen: cabinet color: white; counter-tops: white or cream stone; faucets: Kohler; layout: kitchen island with second sink and bar stools.

The standardization of kitchen decorating is odd given that kitchens are now more open to the rest of the house than they were for the first half of the last century. We've finally made room for easy chatter between chef and couch potato but we don't let the real potatoes hang out on the kitchen countertop. No doubt some deep psychology can explain this. The desegregation of the kitchen from living spaces has created a phobic need to retrench into some spotless, bacteria-free, food operating room.

# Kitchen Taxidermy

As a gesture of protest, the first thing I bought on eBay for my Nantucket kitchen was a taxidermy hen. She is a fine caramel colored hen that came with a clutch of plastic eggs and a basket. Because I happened to be the only taxidermy chicken bidder that day, the lot cost me only $25. In general, I'm not disposed to own a lot of stuffed dead things, but stuffed birds of the sort I might be cooking for dinner seemed all right. Later I bought a taxidermy pheasant for $60 and the two of them sit on a high perch overseeing meal prep and looking out into the back yard, which for all my gardening, still looks like an area you might throw scraps into for your random goat.

If a designer asked about my taxidermy, I could always say they express the traditional barnyard/kitchen rapport that once existed in houses like mine. But really? I bought them as kitchen companions. I look up where they sit on their perch and smile, hoping my renters and future grandchildren will be equally amused. The seller of my taxidermy pheasant emailed me a special offer on a much bigger one, the male mate to mine. Indeed it was more bird for the buck but it frightened me to even look at it on the screen.

Suffice it to say, eBay is a great source for taxidermy, but the wisdom of predetermining your bar on biding prices should also carry over to predetermining your bar on taxidermy purchases. They're cool but at a certain point you appear ghoulish. You wouldn't want that.

# Kitchen Islands

The distance between my kitchen's two walls of cabinets is more than sixteen feet so, skittish about roller skates, I decided to put a workspace in between. On eBay I found an old walnut store counter. It had a handsome paneled front and two expansive shelves on the vendor's side that can hold enough pots, pans and skillets for a summer camp. Slowly but surely, almost all my kitchen equipment has crept out of the cabinets and onto these shelves. There's nothing like turning around from the stove and grabbing a mortar and pestle, juicer, or measuring cup, not to mention a heavy skillet. The seller wisely cross-listed it as a kitchen island, using the same shrewdness as those who list armoires as entertainment centers.

My walnut counter hailed from outside of Chicago. I bought it on Tuesday and by Friday it was waiting to come onto the island via Cape Cod Express—a daily island delivery service. My eBay seller had used one of UShip's drivers and the shipping had cost me all of $100.

It weighs a ton. Recently I checked eBay for "antique store counters" and saw that they abound. Prices range from $200 to the thousands, with plenty in the $350 range.

# Butchering Tables

The previous owners of my house had tucked a small breakfast table and four chairs in the corner of the kitchen. It had such a fifties air about it that it made me want to grab an apron and pour juice. The only significant difference between that fifties breakfast table and our currently popular counter height islands with stools is height.

Which is really all the difference in the world. When I'm cooking, I want my companions to be eye-level or close to it. Height creates equality in the transaction. But if friends and family are seated at a conventional table and I'm standing, then I'm the serving staff; I'm pouring juice.

My walnut store counter couldn't double as a hangout and, like most people, I wanted to make kitchen company comfortable. I decided to create a peninsula on the threshold between the kitchen and a small den. Aesthetically, it would ease the transition between the two rooms. So I searched on eBay for a table to butcher.

Like most antique lovers, I am principled about violating the integrity of an antique . . . most of the time. I would never butcher a nineteenth-century table or a well-designed twentieth-century table, but I would not hesitate to butcher the poorly made or already butchered. Ever since antique farm tables became all the rage, they have become mysteriously plentiful. The clue to this mystery is in the often-incongruous legs. Repurposing old barn siding and floorboards to make a table top is relatively easy. Making a convincing set of legs, not so easy. When I looked up "antique farm tables" on eBay, I knew full well that I would find a number of strumpets and that was what my conscience was searching for. Their genuinely old wood and their $300 to $400 price tag made them a terrific shortcut for my carpenter. He removed the legs at one end, cut the top to fit snuggly around molding and a duct, and extended the two remaining legs to elevate the peninsula to counter-height. Bravo!

If there were a heat map of my house, that table and its four bar stools would be the map's deepest orange. Sketch pads, computers, newspapers, books, maps, coffee cups, shells, glue, broken things, needle and thread, all manner of power cords and connectors need to find their way to that spot for the doing. Because who, really, wants to glue a broken dish alone?

# Dough Bowls and Trenchers

Given my self-righteous indignation at the sterility of modern kitchens, it's obvious that I had to purchase an enormous bowl to put fruit, potatoes, avocados, bags of nuts, and chocolate bars in. It would be the food equivalent to my bookshelves: "Go ahead, grab something," would be the subtext. Dough trenchers are the scale I wanted. They can be 22 to 42 inches long, with a depth that cradles lots of goodies. On eBay they range in price from $45 to $298. The difference seems to be whether or not the seller can prove antiquity. Wooden dough bowls and trenchers with American provenance can be worth a lot of money. Most trenchers are imported from Eastern Europe and Africa. Pottery Barn sells them for $49, a price that includes a tag for nineteenth-century authenticity. Hmmm. So here we are again, fretting

about legitimacy and once again I take a middle ground. I don't like the heavily gouged ones. Besides doubting their post-pubescence, I find them too rough to express love of daily bread, or even love of daily avocado. The ones with smoothed wood and finer surface etchings are more like a grandmother's arms, a fitting cradle. My bowl might have achieved this character yesterday for all I care; with luck, it will get old on my watch.

# Pots and Pans

The prospect of stocking a whole kitchen from scratch made me long for a Macy's Wedding Registry. eBay is the next best thing: a wedding registry's "returns" outlet. Market researchers could learn a lot about what didn't trend this year. It's chilling to think how many "never used" yogurt makers there are in the world.

As usual I became focused on remaking the past (my past) in the form of kitchen equipment I wish I'd put on my 1975 Macy's Wedding Registry. It can be summed up in one word: Dansk. At twenty-two, I was too young to appreciate this Nordic cult. I still thought Revere Ware was the classic pot, so light it would either tip-and-spill or stand-and-burn your food.

To right this past wrong, I could have purchased any number of great brands in cookware: All-Clad; Cuisinart; Calphalon etc.etc. All terrific, all for great prices if you are willing to buy them used. But I decided to enter the eBay time machine and find precisely the mid-1970s Dansk pots, tea kettles, salad bowls, cutting boards, ice buckets, and salad prongs I would have imposed on my wedding guests. And there they all were for a fraction of what they used to cost, without even accounting for inflation.

# The Economy of Sets

Stocking a kitchen with what might have been other peoples' wedding gifts makes you wonder why eBay doesn't create its own registry option. Given that Macy's has replaced George Jensen's and Tiffany's as the go-to destination for wedding shoppers, isn't eBay the next logical step? And so much better because you can find full sets of Limoges and Spode dinner plates and silver flatware, and crystal stemware that don't cost thousands of dollars. (Well, some of the Buy-It-Nows do).

If you're willing to lose a few items in your set, say buy five crystal tumblers not six, you can get a real deal. Not being in the market for crystal and silver, I bought a service for ten of French stainless with plastic or bakelite handles for $45. They're huge (the fork is nine inches long) which is a good thing because on vacation everyone is hungry. I bought a set of six used Bennington trigger handled mugs for $19. For use by renters, I bought a set for six of used Williams – Sonoma Brasserie bowls and plates for $60 and then have added more as bargains surface. For friends and family use I gave myself the pleasure of assembling a collection of antique transferware; they are unmatched but they still get along very well with each other. Three even contain images of Nantucket. If you're patient, you can buy individual mid-nineteenth century plates for $20.

# Placemats and Coasters

Sometimes my heirloom taste smacks of the Harvard Club and nowhere is this more evident than in my preference for cork-backed placemats and coasters. As a child I visited a friend at her grandmother's beach house on Long Beach Island. She had cork-backed placemats with clipper ships on them. A thunderstorm blew rain in on us during dinner. Those are the two things I remember from the visit but only one of them was retrievable on eBay. Now I have those placemats.

The fact that the leading brand of these mats, Pimpernel, has hundreds of listings on eBay, demonstrates how practical they are. They wipe clean. They will survive the estate liquidation. On the other hand it could mean that they are a gift no one really uses. That would explain how many, vintage or used, still come with their box. Is this because they are so handsome they look perishable? Use them!

# Glass Jars and Storage Canisters

We all know that dry goods: rice, flour, sugar, oatmeal and the like, used to be sold in bins at the local store. You'd tell the grocer how much you wanted, he'd scoop it out and weigh it and then pour it into a bag. When you got home, you'd store it in a large jar. We know this because we've seen it in movies and it's what we do at Whole Foods if we're hip.

The most obvious advantage of this practice was economy: the grocer's bulk purchase created a savings that could be passed on to the customer. Not quite so obvious that this is what happens at Whole Foods. My interest in transferring dry goods to jars is not motivated by thrift. First, I like the sound Owens Illinois canisters make when you unscrew their lids. Second is the wonderful feel of their glass ridge pattern in your hand. Third is their forest green color especially in daylight. Fourth is that if food has come in plastic, I want it out of there immediately! Plastic seeps into food; glass and food keep respectfully to themselves.

# American Brilliant Cake Stand

Every Ritz Carlton tea party has cake stands. Why? Because a fancy cake stand is to a cake what high heels are to a leg. Flat on a table, a cake looks good but no one's dancing. Set it on top of an American Brilliant cut glass cake stand and out come the ascots and the cosmetic moles.

It's true that most antique patterned glass is Victorian and that my house is not. But that has never been my rule. My cake stand looks just fine on my rustic farm table with its tin milk bottle caddy centerpiece.

Let every ghost that has ever lived in this house gather round and feel at home.

Search terms for these cake stands begin with "Antique cut glass cake stands." You can add "EAPG" (Early American Pattern Glass) or "American Brilliant."

# Optic Glass Tumblers

When your house has old wavy glass windows, you get used to noticing how glass can act like a painter's brush.

Growing up, I thought Waterford Crystal was the king's crown of whiskey glasses, ice in your hand that held Johnnie Walker on the rocks. But now that I've seen the world through wavy glass, I want to see my scotch that way too. Which means I began searching for "Victorian optic glass tumblers."

The great thing about owning an antique whiskey glass is that you're likely to use it frequently, especially if you are rehabbing an old house. It's important to come to terms with that—with using it. The fact is that you're far more likely to break your wine glasses or even your water glasses. These are props in the frenzy of normal life. Your whiskey glasses are accessories to your deeply meditative, momentarily poetic . . . and then definitely somnolent life ritual.

It took me a while to think of tumbler as a search word. There are a lot of antique eyeglasses on eBay so antique optic glass takes you straight to Benjamin Franklin. "Antique optic whiskey glass" is another option. The tumblers I bought cost me $35 for eight but that was unusual. On the other hand I recently paid $15 for two painted with gold leaf!

# Door Bells and Dinner Bells

A friend of mine has a dinner bell at her back door. She uses it to call in her cats at feeding time. As a child I was called to dinner with a bell. It was a symbol of how untethered we were—wandering the neighborhood like stray cats. Antique store bells can be little wrought iron works of art. My Nantucket doorbell is a nineteenth century hatted gentleman with large brass hands to pull the clanger with.

I found him under "antique iron shopkeepers bell." He arrived caked in black paint. A little scraping revealed his brass face and hands and the brassness of the bell. If sellers are dealers or liquidators, they tend to pass their merchandise along

untouched. As a result they often fail to see the gleam underneath the gunk.

# Portholes

Why is a plug for portholes the last item in the kitchen chapter?

Because we admire it from our kitchen windows. For several years family and friends looked out at the green plank door of my shed. It had strong strap hinges but still . . . a plain door on a utilitarian shed of a shed. Then one day it hit me. It needed a porthole. So I searched "vintage porthole" on eBay and found a terrifically beaten up brass one, with thick glass and a broken latch for $25. Because of its weight the shipping was almost equal to the price. Without removing the door, I drilled four holes to set the perimeter and then jigsawed my way in a circle, connecting my dots. The porthole plunked right in; I screwed it securely through its thoughtfully articulated screw-holes and bingo. It draws your

eye to the back of the yard in the way a dot does and a square does not. But it also has the allure of all ship salvage, as my mentor Underhill knew so well, drawing your thoughts to the sea, the mysterious, wonderful, deep, dark sea.

# 10
## The Road to Paradise

(Is Still Rt 95 in a Rented Truck)

It's an incredible fact that anyone with a driver's license can rent a twenty-six-foot truck and drive it out of a parking lot and onto streets crammed with hapless citizens. No instruction required. The one I rented for my trip up 95 to Nantucket was so long it was parked on a meridian between opposing lanes of traffic. Its sides enhanced with the bubble lettering of a graffiti artist, it looked like a sound barrier-wall. For this reason I didn't take it to be a boon that I'd been "upgraded" from the twenty-two-foot truck I'd ordered. (The clerk's eyes remained fixed on the computer screen the way they do in these circumstances, while only lips move: "None available. None until Tuesday.")

Looking out the window at my truck, I was able to grasp two things at once. First, my truck had been considered too long to easily navigate Penske's parking lot, which is why it was out front. Second, I would not be able to stay in the city overnight because, like Penske, I would never be able to park after loading it. When you're fifty-eight and you've roped all your sixty-something friends into acting out your fantasy of being twenty-one, only in this case your fantasy is most people's worst nightmare of being twenty-one, because it involves rental trucks and heavy lifting up multiple flights of stairs, you hope these kinds of scenes will seem funny. Surely everyone can see how much they'll add to the pleasure of recalling and retelling. But admittedly, there are people who prefer to live in the moment, rather than in some future version of it, and that would include my best friend of thirty-five years, Linda, who was staring out at our truck with gaping mouth and narrowed pupils and summoning a way to say "No" as emphatically as a nice person like her could.

Linda, who, in a moment of succumbing to my enthusiasm, had dubbed our road trip the Return of Thelma and Louise, was now saying there was no way we could manage that truck. Of course she was right. But that hasn't stopped thousands of truck leasers and it wasn't going to stop me, now that I had created a schedule of pick-up appointments with eBayers along a 360-mile stretch

of the Northeast corridor that would make UPS stockholders sell short. Plus I had a freight ferry reservation at 4:30 tomorrow from the Cape. Anyone who's played Nantucket's ferry reservation game knows it doesn't bring out the best in people.

It helped that Jim, another friend, arrived on the scene, looked at the truck and said, "You'll get used to it. Once you get out of the city you'll be fine. In a few hours that willing suspension of disbelief will kick in." Jim had rented his share of moving vans. Some of my friends have had their twenty-one-year-old's budgets longer than others. Jim's has lasted much of his life. I appreciated that.

The new plan was to make our pick-up rounds in Philadelphia and then head out of town at sundown so that we could park for the night in Linda's sumptuous North Jersey driveway. (Forgoing a night of celebrating in Philadelphia). The first stop was my house whose front hall and living room had become a warehouse over the course of two months, the result of more than ten trips to the Greyhound bus station and more than fifty UPS and USPS deliveries. My UPS driver had maintained disciplined disinterest for about the first forty deliveries that included 12-foot rugs, sinks and large oil paintings. A chandelier in a box, whose exposed wrought iron rigging was wrapped in a baby blanket, finally cracked it—a hairline really.

He caught my eye, as he hoisted the fat baby into my awaiting arms, "You have yourself some fun with that." Really . . . how? But maybe I don't want to glimpse the story he had been piecing together these past months.

Another friend joined our team at my house. He apparently has expertise in packing a truck so that not an inch is wasted. A 20 by 38-foot living room full of stuff becomes a three-foot-deep wall on his watch. Never mind that there is no apparent advantage in packing a 3-foot-deep wall of furniture in a 26-foot truck if that's all the furniture you've got. When you're asking friends for help, you take the help that they can give. For that reason, he stayed in the truck constructing a sculpture out of my eBay junk that would have put Louise Nevelson to shame, while we shuttled back and forth, up and down stairs, in and out of the house with heavy loads. When we were finished, there was room for about eight more rounds of the same, or a party. We got some beers.

Stop two was in East Philadelphia, where a queen-sized poster bed I'd bought on Craigslist awaited pick up. When I pulled off Philadelphia's central artery, Vine Street, into the thicket of narrow one-way streets that contained my destination, I understood how a truck is really as useful in a city like Philadelphia as a boat. You might as well just dock at the edge of town and do what you have to do on foot. Which is pretty much what we ended up doing. We slid into a loading zone about three blocks from where the bed resided. As it happened, the trip back with a headboard and footboard was the least of our problems.

The bed owner greeted us sheepishly. She had tried to convince her husband to bring the bed down from the third floor but had failed. We looked at the stair behind her, the usual row house, narrow, railed ratline into darkness, and understood why. "No problem," we said, not having measured the height of the posters against the height of the passageway. We made our way up the stairs, past a child's room spread thickly and evenly with toys, stepping around a laundry basket in transit and a box of shoes that looked permanent, finally arriving at the master bedroom where blinds were still drawn and the bed was a swirl of sheets, as though our arrival had been somewhat disruptive. As we took stock of our cargo, the seller reminded me that one of the railings was broken where it locked into the headboard, the result, she now informed us, of having a 290 pound husband. Roger that.

This was a reminder of why some people are less inclined to purchase used items. In their own minor (or major) way, such purchases force upon us an acquaintance with strangers. Even if the acquaintance is more remote than my standing in front of this woman's unmade bed, even if the acquaintance is only glimpsed in the scratches on a mixing bowl, it is unvetted, unless having a PayPal account is your idea of a club. Many people are too private for that, or, let's just admit it, too elitist. I have my own share of pride and prejudice but these are easily overwhelmed by my propensity to find things amusing and that was certainly the case here. If ever Wikipedia needed an example of TMI this was it. Forever after I am cursed with imagining that fateful plunge and loud crash. But on better days I lie in my big poster bed, just grateful I don't have a 290-pound husband.

Now the trick was to get the bed down the stairs without laughing. Laughing is the worst thing you can do when you're carrying something heavy. It's a muscle softener as sure as Downy.

The next stop was at a friend's house just outside of the city. She had been storing a couch and two chairs, upholstered in a wonderful old chintz, for her ninety-one-year-old mother, who, she was persuaded, might no longer need them since she hadn't needed them for twenty years. Her mother agreed and considered that a house in Nantucket (which she loved) was a worthwhile charity.

True, accepting this gift was not meeting my challenge of buying everything on eBay, but "free" trumps even eBay.

Leaving the labyrinth of the city was a relief, but only until we arrived at my friend's driveway, unpaved and winding deep into woods. Once in, we would not be able to turn around. We would have to go in backwards or exit backwards and it was anybody's guess where the height of the truck would meet branches. Even worse was the fact that the driveway was at the edge of an embankment; its twists and turns offered no forgiving shoulder. I wasn't sure my buddies at AAA could handle a 26-foot truck dangling over a wooded glen on its rear axle. And the driveway was about two tenths of a mile long.

We made it about half way, in reverse. Jim took over when my nerves liquefied. We quit when his did. Once again the rest of the delivery was on foot and the furniture was not inside the door but this time down narrow basement stairs and underneath a stack of other stored treasures awaiting her mother's, what? Second wind? Second coming?

This might be the right time to explain why I had roped my friends into doing this with me. Putting aside thrift, reason number one was that I wanted to share my house with them, really share it, and this was all too clearly legitimate sweat equity. For years we had all played moving men to our children, schlepping back and forth to college, hatchbacks operating like sandwich presses. We were used to being generous, patient, and servile to our children. Now we were back where we started, with friends as family, trying to reconstruct the interdependencies that had made friendships so deep when we were in our twenties. I wanted my friends to feel like Nantucket was their club house.

Even so, it was beginning to dawn on me that loading a behemoth truck and driving it seven hours

up the coast raised the bar on the things we did as friends. As soon as we arrived at Linda's that night I called a handyman I knew on the island and signed him up to unpack the truck once we got there. When I announced this, my friends were oddly sanguine about losing out on that end of the fun.

Linda and I set out early the next day in the truck. Jim would drive my car to Hyannis. That would be our means of returning to Philadelphia, as the truck was a one-way rental. Nobody wants to drive an empty truck 360 miles. Driving an empty trailer is like being tied to an angry stallion. Its bucking will flip you if you're not lucky. A night's sleep had restored Linda's Thelma and Louise enthusiasm for the trip. As we crossed the Tappan Zee Bridge, a haze over the Hudson was beginning to filter the rising sun into shards of gold. I suggested that we tank up and get an Egg McMuffin, an evil pleasure I allow myself on road trips. Only Linda could find that equally thrilling and squeal. We had escaped the high walls of our diet-restricted refrigerators. No way were we going to track down fruit and low-fat yogurt on the New York State Thruway.

Finding an empty aisle of gas tanks, I ball-parked the rear of the truck's proximity to the last hose and got down as usual by swinging outward with the door and dropping to the ground. I swiped my card, grabbed the hose and looked for that little metal cap that should be on the backside of a vehicle. Not there. I swung the hose around to the rear and looked under the license plate. "Any idea where the gas goes on a truck like this?" I called over to an Indian-looking attendant. He continued to pump. I shouted to Linda, who hopped out and retraced my steps. "Maybe there's a manual in the glove compartment." There wasn't. "We can't be the first Penske truck to have pulled into this gas station. Someone here knows where the cap is," I shouted to Linda who was still rustling through the cab for instructions. The attendant sauntered over. "Problem?" I grabbed the hose

again and waved it in circles at the truck.

"You drive this truck?" he asked, trilling his r's so that his parting lips camouflaged a smile struggling to keep from cracking. Silently he departed my company and walked two tanks down to the front of our truck. He reached under the driver's door and unscrewed the cap. "Cash or Card?"

If we'd thought about it, which obviously we didn't, we would have realized that our truck was really a motorized vehicle pulling a lifeless trailer; no motor, no gas tank, it was just a huge wagon. So much for earning the privilege of rolling a cigarette pack into the sleeve of my t-shirt.

Our principal eBay pick-ups were in New Bedford, Massachusetts, and Taunton, Rhode Island. I had already staged a number of earlier runs in New Jersey and New York, including one on Long Island that involved taking a car ferry to Port Jefferson. A set of lovely, scroll-armed nineteenth-century Hitchcock chairs, which now surround my dining room table, had once had a water view. Chairs, like children, are not masters of their fate when it comes to divorces and remarriages. Do my chairs now sulk silently throughout dinner? I doubt it; they look well worn and inured to life's vicissitudes.

I guess it's not surprising that the only state between Philadelphia and Massachusetts that did not involve a pick-up was the one with the highest per capita income—Connecticut. As soon as we felt the road surface move from a whooshing smooth tarmac to a patchy rough concrete, we knew we were back in eBay country. State highway budgets seem always to be inversely related to numbers of eBay traders.

It so happened that some of my New England furniture purchases were from vendors who rent space in antique malls or warehouses. Pick-up was conveniently at the shops, where there was room to load the truck and where there were other hands to assist. My favorite of these was Acushnet Antiques in New Bedford, which I had visited several times before. In fact, if you're looking for the kind of maritime antiques I was buying, you'll often see New Bedford as the eBay seller's location and there's a high probability your seller also has a stall at Acushnet's. It's a huge warehouse on the Acushnet River next to a fish processing facility. When you arrive there, after a long journey from the South, your nose is given a seaside welcome with the intensity of smelling salts.

Like most of these antique cooperatives, the vendors take turns minding the store . . . some more than others. The regulars are a bunch of retirees for whom the store's long counter seems to function like a park bench. They chatter, quip, chuckle, howl, insult, rebuke. If this were France, they would be playing boules in the square, but as it's Massachusetts, they're selling junk and having a good time at it.

A bedroom chest of drawers, and three painted bedside tables were my scheduled pick-up. Carl, the business's owner, gave me a sweet deal on a candle table and a fan-back Windsor chair. eBay purchases are sometimes the equivalent of a loss leader for sellers who can tie "pick-up only" to a store they own. In this case though, Carl's gifts were a loss follower, because, well, he's a very nice guy.

With only an hour to go, Linda was praising my skill at setting in motion such well-calibrated machinery. All three pick-ups had been within minutes of what I'd predicted and we were only an hour from our destination with two hours to spare before ferry time. Which in every way indicated what was about to take place.

In film plotting there is something called a false climax and it's very irritating. Of course, we're no longer fooled by it. We know better than to think that our underdog team will not win the game after all; we know not to trust the antagonist's smiling confidence, and the hero's exhaustion. We know full well that these are deceptions. We will be asked to believe (for precisely six and half minutes) that it's all over, when really we know it's not. The hero will rise again like a phoenix, soul deepened, heart purified, mind sharpened by defeat, and offer up the real climax in which he or she (but usually he), is guaranteed to win.

A false climax is even more aggravating when it occurs in life.

Route 95 in Rhode Island is hilly; Route 195 in Massachusetts is not. It made no sense for my foot to be pressed almost to the floor on a little swell in the road. It made less sense for that to be the case as we moved downhill. The speedometer stabilized at about 45 MPH. I'm used to driving a manual transmission so my automatic response was to shift the truck's drive shaft from "D" to "2." That caused us to lurch in a manner that transformed Linda's complexion. The good news was that the truck continued to move. But truly this was a dumb script. Who would have been so transparent as to write a storyline in which our speed was reduced by a little less than half, precisely the amount that would cause our race to the ferry to be touch and go? If the truck had simply broken down, that would have been a lot more realistic. But the transmission just kept grinding away and we had a chance at making the ferry. This mattered because I doubted I could get another reservation for a truck this large any time soon.

I decided not to share with Linda the footnote that I had been warned about Penske's reputation for poor maintenance. My sources claimed that their tolerance for turning trucks around without engine checks is what enables them to beat UHAUL prices. In spite of this warning, I had gone for the better deal. Call it optimism or arrogance or simple shortsightedness, it's my usual M.O. I knew that Linda would have researched all truck rental companies, checked track records for things like this, and done business with the most reliable company. She would have put safety over thrift. In every way, she is a much better person than I am; witness the fact that I didn't share this with her.

I also didn't share what I knew about the incline of the Bourne Bridge, our access to the Cape. We were moving at an even 45, in the right hand lane, and our spirits had evened out as well. Signs indicating miles to the Cape began to include miles to Hyannis and every time they appeared, Linda looked at her watch, exhaled, and then uttered some chirpy variation on "piece of cake." The bridge appeared over an embankment of trees like King Kong. Linda gasped the way the script indicated. I was struck with an appalling vision of the truck rolling backwards on the bridge. Could it do that without being in reverse? But I strangled the question before it escaped my mouth. There was no way I could speed to gain momentum but I tried.

As we neared the bridge, cars behind us switched lanes well in advance of approaching us. Smart move.

"Okay, lean forward," I commanded. We began to climb. Our speed was slipping slowly but we were still climbing. Drivers in passing cars glowered at me, but hey, I was still climbing. Linda's eyes were so glued to the road ahead I thought she was trying to shoot out some form of telepathic lifeline we could pull ourselves up with, and it was working because we were still climbing. By the summit we were down to 10mph.

We might not have made it another hundred feet but it didn't matter because there we were, 135 feet above sea level, overlooking a beautiful winding canal, a downhill slope and a mound of green spelling out Cape Cod. And that was the end of the false climax, thank God.

The ferry I had booked was not the Steamship Authority's standard car and passenger boat but a freight ferry for commercial trucks. It didn't have much of a sitting area as most trucker's incline toward staying in their cabs and taking advantage of the gently rolling Nantucket Sound. It's a two-hour trip; perfect for an afternoon nap. Jim, his sister Ruth and her son, Peter, who joined us at the dock, Linda and I, crowded around one of two tables in a small room adjoining the pilot's cabin. I handed out beers and a cup of wine for Linda, and within ten minutes, Linda and I partook in the wisdom of our fellow truckers.

The rest of the story is pretty much the same as everyone else's misadventures when trying to move a truckload of furniture into a nineteenth-century house. The queen-sized box spring wouldn't fit up the stairs so we called an architect friend who told us to saw the frame in half and fold it. That worked. We couldn't figure out how to reassemble the twin brass beds tightly enough to keep them from turning into parallelograms so we tied the headboards to the wall. That worked. I had measured curtain lengths assuming windows were consistent in each room (a very stupid mistake given my wonky floors) so I let out some hems. That also worked. But all in all, arranging the furniture seemed more like a ritual than a move, like setting up my Christmas crèche. Every table and chair, like my wise men, sheep, and shepherds, had its designated spot, as though the house, with every generation contributing, had always contained those pieces. It just so happened that every generation contributing was an eBay seller, happy to offer up a well-travelled lamp or two.

Jim and Linda had visited the island before, but Ruth and her son had not. As we drove down Fair Street, Ruth read aloud the house names, "Fair Play"; "Love of Fair"; "Seafairer"; "Fairever"; 'Fair Isle'; "Family of Fair"; "Fairy Tale" . . .

"What will you name your house?" Ruth asked.

"Not a pun," I assured her.

I had been thinking about this, of course. I'd even compiled a list of house names around the island and then classified them. My first inclination was to name the house a term of endearment, one of the many aggregate phrases I call my children: precious lamb; sweet pea; little dream. My son countered with "Guerrilla Unit." I nixed it, but I saw his point. Why be "public like a frog" (to quote Emily Dickenson) about my sentimentalism. Then I thought about making the name more of an invitation and that's when I remembered the refrain from a poem by Quentin Blake: "All Join In." Everyone had already joined in in the making of the house, all my friends, family, and eBay cousins. It had been a real and virtual barn-raising. Now everyone should join in to enjoy it. Isn't that what had already made the house so much fun?

"And if Ferdinand decides to make

a chocolate fudge banana cake

What do we do? For goodness sake!

WE ALL JOIN IN!"

*Blake, Quentin. All Join In. London: Red Fox, 1992.

The Heirloom House